Image Performance
in CRT Displays

Tutorial Texts Series

Image Performance
in CRT Displays

Kenneth Compton

Tutorial Texts in Optical Engineering
Volume TT54

Arthur R. Weeks, Jr., Series Editor
Invivo Research Inc. and University of Central Florida

SPIE PRESS
A Publication of SPIE—The International Society for Optical Engineering
Bellingham, Washington USA

Library of Congress Cataloging-in-Publication Data

Compton, Kenneth.
    Image performance in CRT displays / by Kenneth Compton.
      p. cm. – (Tutorial texts in optical engineering)
    Includes bibliographical references and index.
    ISBN 0-8194-4144-9
    1. Cathode ray tubes–Quality control. 2. Video display terminals–Materials.
    I. Title. II. Series.
TK7871.73.C65 2002
621.3815'422—dc21

                                      2001049883
                                      CIP

Published by

SPIE—The International Society for Optical Engineering
P.O. Box 10
Bellingham, Washington 98227-0010 USA
Phone: 360.676.3290
Fax: 360.647.1445
Email: spie@spie.org
www.spie.org

Printed in the United States of America.

Introduction to the Series

Since its conception in 1989, the Tutorial Texts series has grown to more than 60 titles covering many diverse fields of science and engineering. When the series was started, the goal of the series was to provide a way to make the material presented in SPIE short courses available to those who could not attend, and to provide a reference text for those who could. Many of the texts in this series are generated from notes that were presented during these short courses. But as stand-alone documents, short course notes do not generally serve the student or reader well. Short course notes typically are developed on the assumption that supporting material will be presented verbally to complement the notes, which are generally written in summary form to highlight key technical topics and therefore are not intended as stand-alone documents. Additionally, the figures, tables, and other graphically formatted information accompanying the notes require the further explanation given during the instructor's lecture. Thus, by adding the appropriate detail presented during the lecture, the course material can be read and used independently in a tutorial fashion.

What separates the books in this series from other technical monographs and textbooks is the way in which the material is presented. To keep in line with the tutorial nature of the series, many of the topics presented in these texts are followed by detailed examples that further explain the concepts presented. Many pictures and illustrations are included with each text and, where appropriate, tabular reference data are also included.

The topics within the series have grown from the initial areas of geometrical optics, optical detectors, and image processing to include the emerging fields of nanotechnology, biomedical optics, and micromachining. When a proposal for a text is received, each proposal is evaluated to determine the relevance of the proposed topic. This initial reviewing process has been very helpful to authors in identifying, early in the writing process, the need for additional material or other changes in approach that would serve to strengthen the text. Once a manuscript is completed, it is peer reviewed to ensure that chapters communicate accurately the essential ingredients of the processes and technologies under discussion.

It is my goal to maintain the style and quality of books in the series, and to further expand the topic areas to include new emerging fields as they become of interest to our reading audience.

Arthur R. Weeks, Jr.
Invivo Research Inc. and University of Central Florida

Contents

Chapter 11   IMAGE QUALITY CONTROL AND MAINTAINING PERFORMANCE / 111

Appendix / 115

Index / 117

Image Performance
in CRT Displays

INTRODUCTION

The purpose of this book is to bring a broad spectrum of information related to cathode ray tube (CRT)-based displays into a single easy-to-understand narrative. It requires no working knowledge of a television or how one programs a video cassette recorder (VCR). The starting point of each chapter will be basic information that is followed by detailed explanations and insight into the design trade-offs that influence the image observed. The sequence of topics follows that of a workshop prepared by the author, and the chapters may be read in any order. However, the information in each chapter does build upon the material in the preceding chapters. It should be noted that all references to a cathode ray tube in this book are to only the glass part giving off light in a display. They do not include the entire display or monitor with the associated electronics, a point of confusion at times even within the industry.

All CRTs use glass as a starting point; formulas involved (glass melt) provide the variations in performance. In the 1950s, when big names in television such as RCA, Sylvania, and Philco were working on color CRT technology, they all had the same problem: monochrome glass could not withstand the high voltages required to make color workable. A breakthrough in glass additives solved this shortcoming and made it possible to achieve 4- and 5-megapixel medical displays. The performance properties and safety limits of the various glass melts are discussed in this book as they relate to monochrome applications in medical imaging.

An overview of the architectural differences between color and monochrome CRTs discusses how they are manufactured and the compromises required by their respective design limits. This leads into the subject of electron optics. Here the main focus is on monochrome optics because it provides performance beyond 1k(1000)-line displays.

In addition to the performance of electron optics, the cathode (electron beam source) is examined as a failure mode for all CRTs. The types of cathodes available and their life expectancy are discussed in terms of cost of ownership, with an example calculation. For medical applications, the inability to render full image fidelity is the true failure mode, not the failure of the CRT to emit luminance. The way in which the electron beam is formed and controlled through the optics determines the shape of the pixel and thus the image quality. The influence of electron optics on the CRT gamma and related performance compromises are discussed in conjunction with phosphor selection.

To say the CRT is a mature product is stating the obvious. Sir William Crookes developed the progenitor of the modern electron gun in 1878 as he experimented with variations on the Geisler discharge tube. Then, in 1897, the German physicist Karl Ferdinand Braun demonstrated a tube intended to display

1

electrical waveforms. It was not until 1920 that Vladimir Zworykin of Westinghouse Electric developed the other components needed for the first camera and picture tube, respectively called the iconoscope and kinescope.

In the 1930s the first broadcast architecture was tested using a format that became the standard for North America. The National Television Standards Commission (NTSC) established a format of 520 lines interlaced at 60 Hz refresh rate. Given the level of performance available with vacuum tubes, interlacing the video with odd and even lines was a necessity. In this way, the video amplifier wrote only half the lines with each vertical scan. This in turn kept the horizontal scan rate down to 15 kHz. To this day, an NTSC television displays broadcast signals the same way it did in the late 1940s when commercial television became a reality. Because of other limitations at the time, only about 480 lines of the 520 in the signal can be seen. This is called overscan, meaning that the active video is larger than the viewing space provided. Many control problems could be hidden in the area just outside of what is visible.

Today's color monitors and monochrome medical-grade displays run at frequencies well above those of television and put all the information within the available viewing area. A SVGA boot format of 800 × 600 pixels starts at 30 kHz and climbs to 105 kHz to support 1600 × 1200 at 72 Hz refresh rate. In a medical portrait orientation, 118 kHz is required to support the same pixel format. A five-megapixel (2560 lines) display tops out at 180 kHz. How does this differ from TV technology in terms of design application? A TV set today can be reduced to a handful of integrated circuits (ICs) that include the power output for a number of circuits. The performance required for medical-grade displays is not to be found in a handful of ICs.

Phosphors are more than just a color preference to be based on historical film usage. There are efficacy and long-term aging considerations that determine calibration cycles and the ability to color match old and new displays in multihead workstations. The image quality as defined by the individual pixel requires careful consideration of both the electron optics and phosphor performance. In addition, spatial noise is a factor to be considered with all blended phosphors against the image complexity of the source modality.

It is relatively easy to generate pixels. Being able to resolve them is the key to superior image quality. The metrics involved in defining a pixel and how distortions can influence the net results are illustrated using Microvision scans of both individual pixels and a series of pixels at the Nyquist frequency with two types of optics and video amplifier. Pixel fidelity is also separated into vertical and horizontal aspects of performance, which are controlled by the optics and video amplifier, respectively, in a raster-scanned device. This leads to a net performance as illustrated by a depth of modulation (DMOD) scan for the same optic/video combinations.

Luminance uniformity on a CRT display is generally better than that of an average light box. What contributes to this phenomenon is a multitude of events working against the intended result. Compensation can be utilized, but there is a price to be paid, and how CRT uniformity is defined is still subject to question. Two potential approaches to defining uniformity are reviewed and weighed against uncompensated results.

Compliance with the DICOM grayscale standard display function (GSDF) is reviewed to illustrate how important it is to specify a display's performance with hard numbers, particularly video bandwidth. The background information from the preceding chapters is needed to fully appreciate this discussion.

Test patterns and how to read them for information about a display's performance can prevent second-guessing in the absence of test equipment. Use of the test pattern of the Society of Motion Pictures and Television Engineers and Briggs test pattern 4 as quality assurance tools illustrates the benefits of proper utilization and indicates what is not acceptable. The American Association of Physicists in Medicine (AAPM) Task Group 18 has developed quality control patterns specifically for medical imaging.

The video card, whether it is a commercial graphics or a custom medical card, is part of the video path and should always be tested in conjunction with the intended display. Video card performance varies with manufacturer, and not all digital-to-analog converters are created equal, all of which contribute to the shape of the pixel. Medical-grade cards are discussed with alternative paths using software preprocessing or software compensation based on commercial color cards for monochrome displays.

Acknowledgments

This book would not have been possible without the generosity of Clinton Electronics Corporation in permitting it to be written as part of an internal project that provided access to technical data and CRT manufacturing history spanning 40 years. Many individuals with whom I have had the privilege of working with through SPIE, the Society for Computer Aided Radiology (SCAR), and AAPM are responsible for my understanding of softcopy imaging requirements and how to relate that information to display performance. I thank them, one and all, for their patience and continued support.

Chapter 1

CRT GLASS

Glass formulations (melts) for cathode ray tubes (CRTs) produce some of the highest quality glassware available. This glassware equals or exceeds the finest crystal in lead content and comes very close to being defect free in both contaminant-induced artifacts and optical properties. A glass plant is a 24-hour-a-day, 7-day-a-week operation. The raw materials are relatively inexpensive, but the energy required to sustain tons of molten glass accounts for most of the operating cost. Glass tanks, which are a substantial capital investment, are rated by the tons of glass poured in 24 hours. A small tank would be rated at 10–20 tons and is best suited for smaller-sized glassware to maintain a balance between parts/hour and optimum flow rate.

Molten glass is drawn from the center third of the vertical axis to feed the molds. The top third contains contaminants being burned off, while the bottom third contains heavier particles of raw material that will not melt plus particles from the wear and tear of the firebricks. A continuous pour must be maintained at the tank's rated capacity to maintain the middle third at the proper level within the tank. Once a specific melt formula is established, a usable product can be produced. Glass poured before stability on a new tank is achieved is crushed (collet) and cycled back into the tank at up to 20% of the total raw material. Once a tank is pouring glass, it is preferable to run it without interruption on high-volume parts. But since CRTs come in many sizes, there is a need to change molds. To avoid downtime, glass tanks have multiple taps going to forming stations (turrets with four to six mold sets are typical), so that glass can be poured on two or more stations while the molds are being changed on another station. The mold sizes must be balanced for rate of pour and tonnage to keep the tank flowing within its capacity.

All cathode ray tubes are made from three parts to make a finished CRT as shown in Fig. 1.1: the faceplate, funnel, and neck tubing. (Glass manufacturers refer to the faceplate as a panel.) To transition a tank from one melt to another, such as going from 30 to 42% transmittance, the molds for faceplates must be changed over to funnels or some other glassware that is not critical for optical properties. When the transition is completed, the faceplate molds are phased back in.

The treatment of color and monochrome glassware diverges from this point, based on CRT processing, not the melt. Color CRTs start with two subassemblies, the faceplate and a funnel neck that are flame sealed together. Monochrome CRT processing starts with one piece called a bulb that consists of the faceplate, funnel, and neck tube all flame sealed together. This is how they would arrive at their respective CRT plans for processing.

Figure 1.1 Monochrome CRT.

1.1 Color Glass

The basic building block for glass is one or more oxides of silicon, boron, or phosphorus with certain basic oxide additives. A specific glass melt is identified by what differentiates it from other melts. Color display faceplates are typically made from a lead-free barium–strontium melt. This formula provides nonbrowning characteristics along with a high anode voltage capacity of 24 to 32 kV and is highly absorbent of x rays. The barium–strontium color melt is only utilized for the faceplate. The funnel and neck reverts to a clear potash–soda lead glass that must be physically compatible with the barium–strontium for thermal expansion properties. The potash–soda lead has high x-ray absorbing characteristics. Table 1.1 lists color and monochrome glass melt properties.

The additives (tints) used in color glass enhance the contrast by changing the overall transmittance percent and provide selective transmittance for high color purity (e.g., improved flesh tones on television). Transmittance levels are defined at screen center at 10.16 mm of thickness with a light source of 546 nm. This measurement standard applies to all glass melts. The standard melts for color have transmittances of 86%, 73%, 57%, and 46%. For faceplates thicker than 10.16 mm at screen center, the percent will be lower. An example is the standard 21-inch flat square (FS) diagonal faceplate used in most diagnostic-grade displays: It has 57% glass, yielding a transmittance of 55% owing to the thicker wall.

The progression from the early days of color CRTs with 35–40-inch radius faceplates to the newer FS (60–68-inch radius) and True Flat screens has introduced a variable into luminance uniformity. The FS faceplate has a wedge shape from the center to the edge that causes a 7% change in transmittance for color glass. If the center is at 55%, then the edge of the active video is down to 48%. The transition is gradual and difficult to see unless specific test conditions

Table 1.1 Melt properties of color and monochrome glass.

Glass Properties	
Color CRT Panel Glass	
PT-28C PT-28HG PT-28S PT-28T	Lead-free barium–strontium glass Nonbrowning, high strain point and high x-ray absorbing properties Four types of transmittance: 86%, 73%, 57%, 46% at 10.16 mm, 546 nm Compatible for sealing with color funnel glass
Color CRT Panel Glass with High Color Purity and Contrast Characteristics	
PT-28C PT-28X	Neodymium-doped lead-free barium–strontium glass Nonbrowning, high strain point and high x-ray absorbing Two types of transmittance: 86%, 60% at 10.16 mm, 546 nm Compatible for sealing with color funnel glass
Color CRT Panel Glass for Projection	
PC-28	Lead-free barium–strontium glass Ultra nonbrowning, high strain point and high x-ray absorbing properties High transmittance: 90% at 10.16 mm, 546 nm Compatible for sealing with color funnel glass
Black and White CRT Panel and Funnel Glass	
ST-5KHL ST-5DHL	Tinted barium–lead glass with x-ray absorbing properties Two types of transmittance: 42%, 30% at 10.16 mm, 546 nm
Color CRT Funnel Glass	
FT-22H	Clear potash–soda lead glass High strain point, high x-ray absorbing properties and electrical resistivity
Color CRT Neck Tube	
L-35	Clear potash–soda lead glass High strain point, high x-ray absorbing properties and electrical resistivity Compatible with color funnel glass
Black and White CRT Neck Tube	
L-29	Clear potash–soda lead glass High electrical resistivity and x-ray absorbing (lower strain point than L35)

Source: Glass codes are from Nippon Electric Glass Co., Ltd. Codes are specific to the glass manufacturer. An alternative glass source designation for monochrome in standard tint is T42 and in a dark tint is T30, corresponding to ST-5KHL and ST-5DHL, respectively.

are used. The curvature of the glass on the outside and inside is not a single radius, so the rate of change in transmittance is not the same in all directions. The main benefit of a flatter faceplate is the improved reflective characteristics. Less illuminance is directed back toward the eye because the larger radius has a reduced lens effect. Older 30-inch radius CRTs concentrated illuminance and were referred to as having a headlight effect. The flatter generation reflects more incident illuminance below the level of the eye.

1.2 Monochrome Glass

A tinted barium–lead glass with x-ray absorbing characteristics though is used in both the faceplate and funnel glass. Anode capacity is limited to approximately 21 kV at a diagonal size of 21 to 23 inches. Smaller diagonal sizes would have to operate at lower anode voltages. The lead in monochrome glass is what turns brown when the glass is exposed to high-energy x rays. Keeping the anode voltage below 21 kV and limiting the beam currents prevents this from becoming a failure mode. In general, the cathode will be depleted before glass browning becomes an issue on large CRTs. The image quality for diagnostic reading would also be questionable long before glass browning was observed.

Glass melts for monochrome are 42% (standard) and 30% (dark) at 10.16 mm thickness and 546 nm. A clear monochrome melt has been used in the past at 90%, but the benefits are minimal when color glass in the same bulb size is available.

Like color, monochrome started out with 35–40-inch radius (1R bulbs for black and white television, B&W TV) faceplates that had a fairly uniform wall thickness from center to edge. Flat square bulbs are also poured with monochrome glass melts (also called flat profile, depending on the source). With standard tint glass and the same wedge-shaped profile, the 21-inch FS faceplate will now cause a 15% drop in center-to-edge transmittance; the standard 42% tint glass yields 34% at screen center in this bulb design. This represents the worst-case example of luminance nonuniformity that is due to the thickness of the glass.

The neck tube for monochrome glass is also a clear potash–soda lead glass, but with slightly different coefficients in order to be compatible with the barium–lead funnel. The high electrical resistivity of the neck glass is important in containing the anode voltage around the electron optics (also called a gun mount in the CRT industry).

1.3 Glass as an Insulator

An operating CRT is a large capacitor with stored energy. The glass is the dielectric material separating the opposing charges. The inside is charged to a positive voltage (anode potential) and the outside is tied to chassis ground points. As a dielectric, glass is not conductive, but it will allow a surface charge to be established. The first B&W TVs had no aluminum backing on the inside surfaces and the TV took a long time to produce luminance by today's standards; i.e., it took time to build up the anode voltage as a surface charge. The outside surface of the funnel, the other half of the capacitor, is coated with Aquadag to provide conductivity to ground; Aquadag contains graphite particles in a paintlike (water-based) vehicle. The application of Aquadag solved a high-voltage stability and capacity shortcoming when high-voltage circuits were all tubes. The Aquadag helped stabilize what would otherwise have been fluctuations in anode potential, causing fluctuations in luminance and picture size.

Today there is aluminum backing on the inside of monochrome CRTs that provides a conductive surface on the funnel. Color utilizes a conductive funnel coating that can be sprayed on. Both color (typically) and monochrome use aluminum backing for the phosphor screen. In addition to conductivity, it provides a protective layer for the phosphor, a heat sink, and a reflective surface to direct luminance outward. Aquadag still provides the ground plane on the outside, but is not needed to support modern high-voltage power supplies that are more robust and stable.

Glass can lose its dielectric properties with excessive heat and thus lead to a failure of the CRT. This is not very common because modern display designers are very conscious of heat management. One of the major heat sources within a display is the deflection yoke, and its design involves more than geometry and focus integrity. It must also run as cool as possible to avoid elevating the glass temperature under the yoke. The yoke is positioned where the neck and funnel glass come together. The yoke coils are over the thinner neck glass and joint (splice) with the funnel. Design engineers must measure the glass temperature when testing any new yoke design.

At 75°C, the ion mobility of the glass structure begins to increase, which reduces the insulating characteristics. Most CRT manufacturers would recommend that the "glass" temperature remain below 90°C and preferably below 85°C. Above 100°C, the properties have changed sufficiently to risk arcing from the anode potential to the yoke windings. Arcing erodes the glass and, if allowed to continue, will punch a hole through the neck glass, venting the CRT to the atmosphere. Above 120°C, the glass has lost most of its insulative properties and arcing will be heard as a "tick-tick-tick" sound.

1.4 Usable Area

The glass plant and the CRT manufacturer use a variety of dimensions, all of which are correct if they are applied in context. Glass plants define a bulb by the outside dimensions of the faceplate (panel) between opposite (diagonal) corners. The screen area is the surface area available for phosphor to be applied as defined by the glass plant. Not all standards are acceptable in all countries, and bulbs may also be designated with a "V" following the dimension, which denotes the viewable diagonal measure. For instance, what is called a 21-inch diagonal CRT in one country would be a 20V in another.

The actual area available to present information is the "active video area," which the display manufacturer will specify. This is the area that counts because two display manufacturers may use the same CRT but provide different active video areas. The difference can be significant and may be caused by a number of design compromises.

The video should not be extended fully into the corners and edges of the CRT. The bezel opening surrounding the CRT should be sized to deny this option to the user. Optical distortions will occur as the active video area reaches the inside transition radius at the edges (the inside radius of the faceplate wraps around to the side, called the skirt). The image will follow the curvature and be outside of the display's ability to maintain geometry and focus. In this same area is a characteristic feature of the molding process called suck-up. It is caused during the mold release phase and it leaves a ridge of glass like a bead in varying degrees that will behave the same as a lens. The active video area should always be defined to avoid these problems by remaining clear of the transition radius.

1.5 Contrast Enhancement

The darker the tint (i.e., the lower the transmittance percentage), the greater the contrast enhancement potential. However, this gain must be judged against the increase in drive required to achieve equal luminance and the impact on beam size. The de facto standard diagnostic display is a 21-inch FS bulb using color glass melt at 55%. This does not provide a desirable level of contrast enhancement, so a secondary tinted panel of 62% or 90% is bonded to the faceplate. The net transmittance becomes 34% and 50%, respectively. These panels should also have an antireflective coating to further enhance contrast. For a standard 21-inch FS monochrome melt at 34%, a 90% panel nets 30% transmittance and meets most requirements.

The ambient conditions for a workstation influence the choice to be made. In high ambient conditions the display must overcome more illuminance. The 62% panel would make this more difficult, while the 90% would permit greater luminance. In a dark reading room the darker panel would provide a better balance.

Contrast enhancement by the CRT faceplate works on a simple principle. The luminance energy from the phosphor passes through the faceplate only once, being attenuated by the stated percentage. For ambient light, some is reflected at the surface of the glass and observed as glare while the balance enters the glass to be reflected by the inside glass surface and phosphor screen, thus being attenuated twice, on the way in and on the way out. Secondary reflections within the glass would be attenuated multiple times.

1.6 X-Ray Compliance

Color and monochrome glass have different operating limits owing to the glass melt characteristics. Regardless of melt, the limit for all CRT displays that must not be exceeded is 0.5 mR/h throughout the useful life of the tube when it is operated within regulation limits of a hypothetical power supply with a 5-MΩ internal impedance. The CRT manufacturer is required to publish International Standards Organization (ISO) exposure rate limit curves for each CRT configuration at a maximum anode voltage and 250 μA of anode current.

A 21-inch FS monochrome melt has an absolute maximum of 24.5 kV anode voltage.[1] The recommended operating range for a typical configuration is 18 kV to 21 kV. At 21 kV, the anode current could be as high as 1200 μA and be within the 0.5 mR/h limit. A 340 cd/m^2 (100 fL) display would peak at just over 300 μA, one-fourth of the limit. The 21-inch FS color counterpart has a maximum of 37 kV anode voltage.[2] The recommended operating range for a typical configuration is 25 kV to 28 kV. At 28 kV, the anode current is off the chart in excess of 2000 μA and within limits. The performance increase using color glass at 340 cd/m^2 would reduce the beam current below the monochrome FS, which is again well under the ISO limit curves. The faceplate provides an excellent barrier to x-ray energy and typically yields the lowest readings on the CRT; the neck area is the highest in most designs and operating conditions.

Compliance with the ISO limit curves is the responsibility of the display manufacturer; it must certify the proper use of the CRT in the display's design. Testing is conducted through recognized independent laboratories and reported to the Department of Health and Human Services (DHHS) in the United States and in accordance with the Federal Performance Standards for Television Receivers (21 CFR, Subchapter J). The measurements are done in accordance with the EIA publication No. RS-501 (current version). Display manufacturers also verify compliance on production units in accordance with good manufacturing procedures and the agencies they are tested under.

References

1. Clinton Electronics Corporation, CRT model A57.
2. Clinton Electronics Corporation, CRT model A18.

Chapter 2

CRT ARCHITECTURES

This chapter discusses the different types of color CRTs and basic monochrome construction. The obvious difference is thousands of potential colors versus a single monochromatic image. In that sense, monochrome becomes an application-specific display device as opposed to a general-purpose one. Buried within the basic architectural differences are performance issues that influence the suitability of one color format over another and the trade-offs involved, as well as the differentiating attributes with monochrome.

All CRTs share a few things in common in the way they produce luminance energy. They must provide a source of electrons that can be controlled over a range of current flow. They must accelerate the electrons to deliver kinetic energy to the phosphor and be able to focus those electrons to a small spot at the center of the screen. The CRT is not responsible for bending the electron beam to fill in the remaining screen area. That comes from the supporting circuits and the deflection yoke mounted on the CRT.

The electron beam source is the cathode. Various types are utilized and the performance issues will be covered later. The common thread is that the cathode has a finite amount of electrons to give up and they are forced from the cathode material by heat (thermionic) and electrical fields (attraction). The filament underlying the cathode structure provides the heat at 800 °C for the older barium-oxide style and up to 1000 °C for dispenser types. Barium-oxide cathodes were subsequently improved by adding scandium doping that extended the useful life by approximately 15% over the barium-oxide-only cathodes. The comparison, however, is very dependent on the manufacturing source of the cathodes.

The filament is specifically designed to support a cathode temperature when powered at either 6.3 V ac or 12 V dc. The most commonly used is 12 V dc because it is already available in most power supplies. A 6.3 V ac tap would require additional electronics. Historically, the 6.3 V ac filament dates back to vacuum tubes and car radios when the car electrical systems were 6 V. Cathode temperature aside, for medical imaging applications, only the dispenser type should be considered.

The angle through which the beam will be deflected to fill the active video area is expressed in degrees measured between opposite corners (diagonal) to the yoke reference line, the approximate location of where the neck tubulation and funnel glass are joined. Color CRTs are dominated by 90-deg funnels with more recent products approaching a 100-deg deflection angle. Color CRT performance would be more difficult to maintain at higher deflection angles because of the increase in deflection distortions and interaction of the three beams (red, green, and blue, RGB). Monochrome with a single beam can be deflected to 110–114 deg to achieve a small front-to-back footprint, but at the expense of spot performance at the edges. The ideal CRT profile for both formats would be a very shallow deflection angle with a footprint unacceptable for the user. Less bending of the beam provides better spot performance over a greater active video area. Faceplates and funnels can be matched up (assuming molds exist) so that a 21-inch FS bulb can be made with either a 110- or 90-deg funnel. The difference is footprint verse optical performance being compromised.

Once the beam has been deflected, it is in the drift space defined by the funnel area and near maximum velocity. Outside influences such as strong magnetic fields (as in magnetic resonance imaging, MRI) or more subtle ones coming from electrical conduits (3ϕ, 208-V ac elevator and office lighting grids) can influence the beam's trajectory. In monochrome, they distort only the geometry; in color, they distort geometry and color purity. Color CRTs use internal magnetic shielding to minimize this potential, while monochrome does not. Color purity is a more immediate visual problem than geometry, particularly when color coding of information is intended.

Monochrome and color differ in physical structure and pixel performance at the point of electron beam impact on the phosphor screen. Those differences and how they relate to what the viewer sees are discussed separately.

2.1 Color CRT Mask

The term "mask" has become a generic term for shadow mask, slot mask, and aperture grill, but the structures differ and provide variations in performance. The two primary systems used in alphanumeric and graphic imaging are the aperture grill and shadow mask as shown in Fig. 2.1. The aperture grill is made up of vertical wires (under tension) between which the three beams converge and pass between to land on their respective color phosphors. By definition, the vertical line count is limited only by the ability of the electronics and optics to produce (write) the scan lines. The phosphor stripes are continuous and only interrupted by two horizontal stabilizing wires that are nearly invisible. The dot pitch defines the horizontal pixel count.

The shadow-mask design uses an Invar alloy with holes through which the three beams must pass. The mask must support its own weight from the edges without mechanical distortion, which would cause color purity and convergence problems. This structural difference between the grill and shadow-mask configurations results in an efficiency difference. The mask has more surface area at anode potential absorbing electrons before they reach the phosphor. The shadow mask absorbs approximately 80% of the electron beam energy. The aperture grill absorbs approximately 70%. The typical maximum luminance specified with a grill approaches 135 cd/m^2 (40 fL), while the mask would be closer to 100 cd/m^2 (30 fL) assuming both had equal video drive capability. To achieve this luminance, the cathode is driven at milliamperes so that microamperes reach the phosphor.

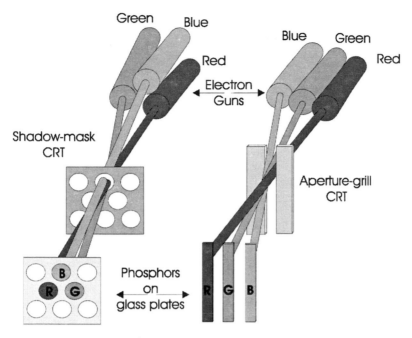

Figure 2.1 Primary masking systems.

Industrial graphics uses such as computer-aided design (CAD) favor the aperture grill for the sharpness of lines and brighter images. The shadow mask is chosen for alphanumeric presentation because the triad of phosphor dots is laid down at an angle 30 deg from the vertical, as shown in Fig. 2.2. This helps to smooth out the stair step (structured) appearance associated with angular lines and curved edges of text.

Both formats have an underlying limit of pixel locations. The dot pitch represents the distance between like color stripes or dots. For the grill this is a straightforward measurement between vertical stripes of like color. The shadow mask is the linear distance between like colors on different horizontal lines. In Fig. 2.2 this is noted as 0.26 mm. The typical dot pitches are 0.25 mm for a grill and 0.26 mm for a shadow mask, putting both formats at roughly 100 dpi (dots per inch) of pixel density. Recent designs also have variable dot pitches and aperture sizes to compensate for inherent edge distortions that are due to beam deflection.

The active video area as determined by the mask in this case will be the limiting factor on pixel density (format). In much the same way as an active matrix, liquid crystal display (AM-LCD) has a specific number of windows (red, green, and blue subpixels) per inch, so does a color CRT. The pixel format from the video source should therefore closely match the actual number of pixel locations. Moiré interference can be anticipated with a mismatch between video source (addressable) and available pixel locations (mask format). Moiré appears

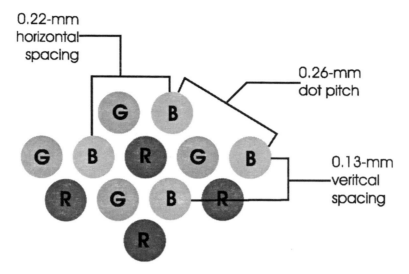

Figure 2.2 Position of phospher dots in a shadow mask.

like a distorted rainbow floating within the glass structure. The mismatch of the video source and mask format beat together and produce the closely spaced lines of the rainbow.

Electron backscatter occurs in all CRTs, but most noticeably in color. Some electrons striking the mask bounce off and land elsewhere, while some of those hitting the phosphor also bounce off and interact with the mask again. The net result is that luminance energy is generated in areas outside of the intended pixel location. This is equivalent to increasing brightness or having diffuse light hit the screen and thus reduce contrast modulation.

Beyond image quality, operating conditions have an impact on selection. Subjecting the aperture-grill configuration to vibrations can induce unwanted distortions if the grill wires respond. A shadow mask would be immune to vibration of the same intensity. An example is an ultrasound cart being bumped and disturbing the color purity until the wires settle down. Color purity is a function of each electron gun hitting only its phosphor color; e.g., the red beam should land only on red phosphor dots or stripes. This is controlled with magnets when the CRT is matched to the deflection yoke. Not all of the electron energy lands on target and this can be seen with a solid field of one color. The red hue will shift from the center to the edge as contributions from the blue and green are added into the mix. Color purity at screen center cannot realistically be maintained across the entire screen area when three electron beams are involved.

2.2 Monochrome CRT

Monochrome CRTs have no mask, which immediately drops the beam current to microamperes for equal luminance with color. The added efficacy allows monochrome to operate at twice the luminance output of color and not be limited by the mask dot pitch determining the pixel format. Beneficial attributes come at a price; in this case, it is control of the electron beam. The electron optics and video amplifier determine the beams shape and ultimately the pixel's quality; there are no shortcuts to making this part work properly.

Like color, monochrome utilizes a backing to protect the phosphor, and this would be aluminum in almost all cases. A slug of aluminum about the size of a long grain of rice will coat the inside of a 21-inch CRT from the faceplate to the yoke reference line. The phosphor screen is sandwiched between the aluminum and faceplate glass, and the amount of phosphor must be controlled. A 21-inch FS bulb has about 6 g of phosphor adhering to the glass. (Phosphor crystals are deposited by sedimentation in a Kasal medium. Kasal coats the crystals and functions like glue.) The thickness of the phosphor screen is important to pixel quality, especially for diagnostic-grade displays.

The terminology within the CRT industry for specifying the amount of phosphor to be deposited in grams per square unit (centimeter or inch) is screen weight. The resultant thickness of phosphor influences the Gaussian distribution of luminance energy. A thick screen will force light generated at the back of the screen to pass through more crystals to reach the faceplate, thus providing more opportunity for light scattering. A thin screen is less durable than a thicker screen, but the pixels will be smaller at equal current. Six grams in a 21-inch FS is a compromise of durability and pixel size. Screen weight is important to color CRT processing as well, but the inherent performance of a color CRT will mask it.

2.3 CRT Mechanicals and Safety System

All CRTs operate with an internal vacuum of 10^{-7} torr or greater. During the life of the product, the atmosphere is trying to get inside. To resist this pressure, the bulb designer has to incorporate physical strength into an oddly shaped vessel while achieving the desired viewing function. Today's flat CRTs have the advantages of finite element analysis to test concepts before the tool steel for a mold is cut. The result is that your television, personal computer monitor, or medical display does not need a safety implosion shield bonded to the faceplate as many old B&W TVs and early color sets required.

Safety criteria fall within the purview of the Underwriters Laboratories (UL) and their counterparts around the globe. A CRT manufacturer must submit samples of its product, which are intentionally broken under various conditions; the manufacturer will also pretest the product prior to submission. The rules and conditions are too extensive to be covered here, suffice it to say that other than a few chips from an impact, very few parts of the CRT or none should exit the cabinet. Testing is performed on the faceplate, funnel, and neck glass for failure propagation.

Figure 2.3 Mounting systems from one-piece shrink bands at the top to individual corner ears that would be held on with strapping at bottom. (Courtesy of Clinton Electronics Corporation.)

All CRTs have a mounting system so they can be mounted into the chassis. Older sets had a frame to support the CRT. Modern sets use the CRT as an integral part to support the plastic cabinet parts. What is not obvious is that the strapping around the CRT faceplate skirt is an implosion safety device. It is a convenient place to attach mounting hardware at the corners, but it also provides a compression load on the glass. Figure 2.3 illustrates the diversity of mounting options available to meet the mechanical interface of today's cabinets.

The most common system is strapping (also called banding) used with stamped mounting ears shown in the lower half of Fig. 2.3. The strapping is preheated and tensioned around the bulb and then spot welded in place. The cooling-off process adds the remaining tension, compressive load. A cushioning tape is under the strapping to protect the glass. An alternative mounting system is a die-cut frame (shell bond) that is bonded to the glass with an expanding adhesive, again applying a compressive load. A third alternative is a shrink band (middle of Fig. 2.3) that is heated and slipped over the bulb; cooling provides the total compressive force.

A 21-inch FS has approximately 200 pounds of tension before the strapping cools off. The desired mechanics of a CRT failure when it is hit on the faceplate is for the venting to atmosphere to occur in the funnel region away from the point of impact. The compression load on the faceplate from the strapping causes a crack starting at screen center to propagate and accelerate at near the speed of sound to the edge and onto the funnel where the glass is thinner. Before the faceplate crack can penetrate the wall, it has reached the thinner glass funnel and the CRT is vented from behind the faceplate.

Medical-grade displays should include antireflective coating (ARC) for image enhancement. The typical method of application is to bond a glass panel to a faceplate that has an AR coating. Although it is not necessary for safety reasons, the added panel adds one more level of safety to an already reliable system.

Chapter 3

ELECTRON OPTICS

There have been numerous designs over the past five decades, from the first commercial B&W TVs to the current offering of high-definition televisions (HDTV). As much as they change, the fundamentals dating back to 1878 are still there. An electron cloud is formed, metered out through a control grid, accelerated, shaped, and accelerated again before being turned loose in the direction of the phosphor screen. This process uses electrons that prefer to be separated from each other and surrounds them with strong positive fields without pulling them farther apart.

Depending on the task at hand, a set of problems can be approached with different design solutions. A projection system is a very high drive application with moderate sized pixels on a 7- or 9-inch diagonal CRT. A similar 7-inch photographic system has a very low drive and very small pixels. A 5-megapixel 21-inch medical display requires a fraction of the projection brightness, albeit still bright, but over a much larger area, with pixels approaching photographic requirements. The respective electron optics for these systems are not interchangeable.

Color optics parallels the mask configuration in that the shadow mask utilizes the deltoid (triangular) positioning of the cathodes (three beams) while the aperture grill (and slot mask) utilizes in-line (horizontal plane) positioning. Monochrome optics has a single cathode (one beam) that is centered in the gun mount (a term for the total optical package). Two basic types of monochrome gun mount are used and will be treated separately.

For ease of discussion, only the monochrome mount will be used for explanation. The forces working within a gun mount are complex enough with one beam, and compounding the lines of force in a color mount would require an extensive discussion.

3.1 Basic Structures

Figure 3.1 indicates the location of the heater, cathode, and control grids in a CRT.[1,2]

The heater (H) is a spiraled wire element coated with an insulating material to prevent shorting to the cathode structure. It is designed to maintain a specific temperature of the cathode. Only the lead wires are shown at the base of the gun mount. The heater is located within the cathode cup assembly.

The cathode is in the shape of a cup suspended within a sleeve. The cup is supported by a combination of ceramic and metal structures designed to stabilize the cathode temperature by controlling thermal conductivity. The cathode (K) provides a continuous supply of electrons that form a space charge, i.e., an electron cloud, in front of the emitter surface. The emitted electrons have

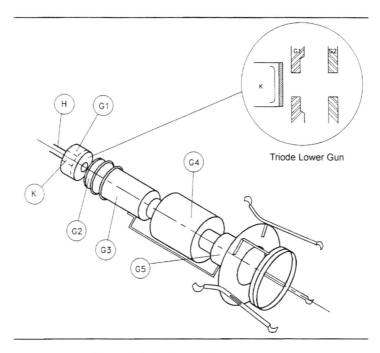

Figure 3.1 Basic structure of a CRT.

a Maxwellian thermal-velocity distribution in each of the axial and radial directions, which limits the spot size that can be attained in any CRT. The design must take into consideration the thermal expansion characteristics of the materials so that critical tolerances are maintained from a cold start through warmup to final operating temperature.

The G_1 control grid is the valve that controls electron flow. It is always negative in potential relative to the cathode and prevents the G_2 electrical field from penetrating the cathode space. This makes it possible to control the amount of current drawn from the space-charge cloud. For any G_2 voltage, there is a minimum negative voltage, that is, a spot cutoff voltage that when applied to G_1 produces visual extinction of the undeflected spot.

The G_2 grid is the first anode (also called the preaccelerator or buffer anode) in old TV nomenclature, but has since lost the longer titles and is now just G_2. It is always positive in potential relative to the cathode and serves two purposes: to accelerate the beam as it exits G_1 and to prevent the higher potential fields of the lens from penetrating into the G_1 space. This blocking attribute permits the display designer to select an anode voltage from the range available in accordance with the CRT manufacturer's recommendations without the need to change the CRT grid spacing.

The aforementioned elements are all part of the lower gun structure known as the triode (see triode inset to Fig. 3.1). The spacing between elements is

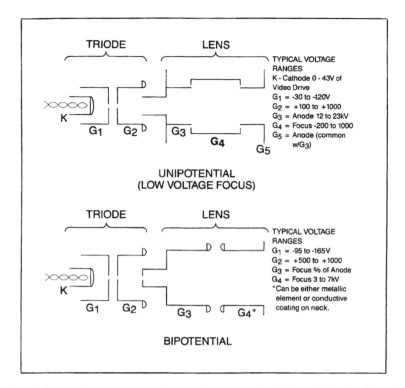

Figure 3.2 Schematic representation of the unipotential and bipotential electron optics.

critical for determining the cutoff voltage range and lower gun beam angles (alpha angle), all of which contribute to the quality of the individual pixel.

The upper gun structure is the lens, and it is composed of two or three elements, depending on the type, as shown in Fig. 3.2. In either case, they are sequentially numbered starting with G_3. A unipotential (low voltage focus) configuration has three elements, with the G_3 and G_5 mechanically linked together and at the same potential as the high voltage (HV) anode. G_4 is the variable focus element, which will adjust the focal length of the beam for the position on the screen, i.e., provides proper focus center to edge. Unipotential is a reference to the G_3 and G_5 being at a common potential. Variations of the unipotential design using higher focus voltages are called either high unipotential or high bias guns.

The second configuration is a bipotential utilizing a G_3 and G_4 element. G_4 can also be the inside surface of the neck glass instead of a metal element. This has the advantage of increasing the through-clearance (internal lens diameter), but at the risk of introducing abnormalities due to distortions in the glass surface (such as being out of round). The name bipotential is in reference to the G_3 and G_4 being at two distinctly different potentials.

The anode (second anode in old TV terms) is at the view screen to accelerate electrons to their final velocity. Internal aluminizing and/or conductive coatings carry this potential back to the neck for a mechanical connection to the gun mount. In a unipotential, this puts the G_3 and G_5 at the same voltage potential as the view screen. In a bipotential, this would be only the G_3 element but through a dropping resistor so that the potential is a percentage of the anode voltage. G_4 is the focus grid, the same as G_4 in a unipotential gun, except that the voltage range is in thousands of volts instead of hundreds. Bipotential guns have excellent beam current handling capacity and generally exceed their unipotential counterparts of the same diameter. They are, however, more sensitive to bending distortions and typically are not found in CRTs with more than 90 deg of diagonal deflection angle.

Color guns will have elements that share a common mechanical structure, but with independent control of cutoff and acceleration in the lower gun structure. The upper gun structure can be more open in the sense that all three beams can be influenced uniformly for focus and final acceleration. They can also have additional elements for fine-tuning the individual beam paths.

3.2 Lower Gun Structure (Triode)

CRT setup criteria provide a rather wide range of biasing alternatives for the display designer. The most common drive arrangement is to apply video drive to the cathode. An alternative is to drive G_1, but this is less efficient in terms of volt drive for beam current achieved at equal cutoff settings. A video G_1 drive does improve control of focus over the full dynamic range, but at the high drive conditions required for medical displays, the trade-off is not practical.

In any CRT, the optimum cathode current can be calculated using one of three possible formulas. Regardless of which one is used, the relationships among the various parameters can be displayed with the same graphic presentation shown in Fig. 3.3.

The Greek symbol for gamma (γ) is unfortunately used in two different ways regarding CRT performance, causing confusion when it is taken out of context. To a CRT optics designer, gamma is the drive fraction, not the gamma response associated with calibration to DICOM (Digital Imaging and Communications in Medicine) using a look-up table (LUT).

The drive fraction gamma, expressed as the drive voltage V_D divided by the cutoff voltage V_C, is the parameter that most severely affects tube performance in guns without limiting apertures.[3] The radius at the cathode from which current is drawn is roughly proportional to γD, where D is the G_1 aperture diameter. Excessive values of γ increase the beam's initial size as well as its size at the crossover point (station 2 in Fig. 3.4) and thereby increase the aberration in the triode lens system. The aberration is proportional to the third power of the beam diameter for a given gun. Aberrations also depend on the relationship of

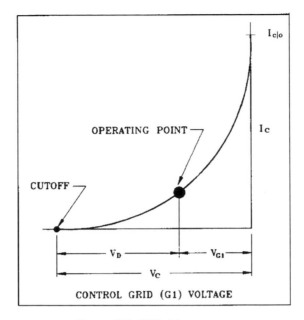

Figure 3.3 CRT drive curve.

the beam diameter to the lens system's inside diameter. As a result, excessive drive levels are the major cause of deterioration in spot size.

The other gamma that is associated with a LUT for DICOM Part 3.14 Grayscale Standard Display Function (GSDF) is the one that comes to mind for most people. The drive fraction gamma does not pertain to the total electronic path that the analog video signal passes through. The GSDF gamma is expressed as Luminance $= K E^\gamma$, where K is a constant, E is the drive voltage above cutoff, and γ is the exponent representing gamma. Gamma should be measured at several drive levels using the formula

$$\frac{L_2}{L_1} = \left(\frac{V_d 2}{V_d 1}\right)^\gamma, \qquad (3.1)$$

where volts drive $V_d 1$ and $V_d 2$ are expressed in relationship to luminance L_1 and L_2, with gamma being the dimensionless variable. Using Fig. 3.3 as a reference, any two points selected to the left of the operating point will yield a considerable difference in the response of the CRT to drive voltages in addition to where the operating point is located. No CRT would be operated at the $I_{C/O}$ bias, full drive condition; the beam would be too large to control.

All the tolerances in a gun mount are critical for consistent performance, but none so much as the triode, where a one-thousandth of an inch (0.025 mm) change in cathode-to-G_1 spacing can produce a change in cutoff of approximately 30%. The spacing chosen by the CRT designer is intended to deliver

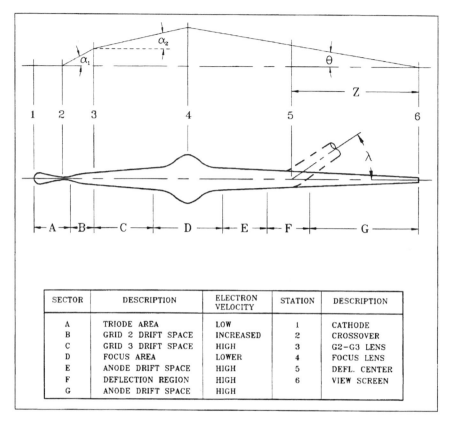

Figure 3.4 Cross-section profile of an electron beam as it travels through the optics.

SECTOR	DESCRIPTION	ELECTRON VELOCITY	STATION	DESCRIPTION
A	TRIODE AREA	LOW	1	CATHODE
B	GRID 2 DRIFT SPACE	INCREASED	2	CROSSOVER
C	GRID 3 DRIFT SPACE	HIGH	3	G2–G3 LENS
D	FOCUS AREA	LOWER	4	FOCUS LENS
E	ANODE DRIFT SPACE	HIGH	5	DEFL. CENTER
F	DEFLECTION REGION	HIGH	6	VIEW SCREEN
G	ANODE DRIFT SPACE	HIGH		

performance and flexibility across product lines. To truly optimize a CRT for a specific application requires the display and CRT designer to work closely together to achieve custom spacing and bias voltages. Doing so would require extremely tight tolerances in the optics that is not practical in volume production.

In Fig. 3.4, the area defined by stations 1, 2, and 3 is the triode. Alpha (α) angles 1 and 2 are design points controlled by the physical spacing between the parts and biasing voltages. The proximity of G_1 to the cathode determines cutoff; the gap between G_1 and G_2 also influences cutoff and the first crossover point. The formation of the beam at this location determines the spread into the G_4 lens, which in turn determines the theta (θ) angle at the view screen. A shallow theta angle produces a softer image, while a steeper theta angle brings the beam into more of a pointed cone shape and sharper focus. The softer image will have less deflection distortion but not necessarily better focus quality. As noted earlier, the inside through-clearance diameter of the lens is important but is limited by the available space (neck diameter). The beam diameter through the lens should remain at less than 10% of the clearance to avoid unwanted radial aberrations.

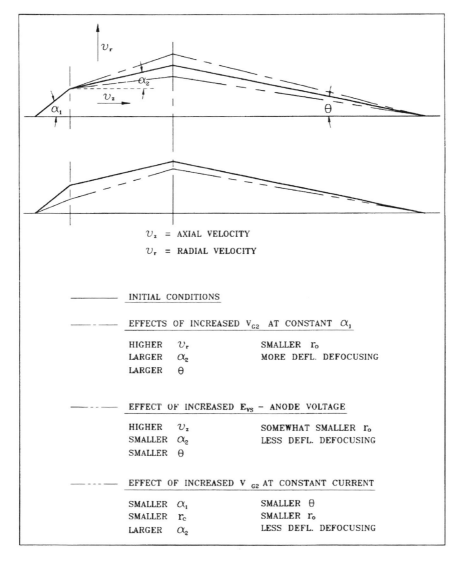

v_z = AXIAL VELOCITY
v_r = RADIAL VELOCITY

_____ INITIAL CONDITIONS

_ · _ · _ EFFECTS OF INCREASED V_{G2} AT CONSTANT α_1

HIGHER	v_r	SMALLER	r_0
LARGER	α_2	MORE DEFL. DEFOCUSING	
LARGER	θ		

_ · · _ EFFECT OF INCREASED E_{VS} – ANODE VOLTAGE

HIGHER	v_z	SOMEWHAT SMALLER	r_0
SMALLER	α_2	LESS DEFL. DEFOCUSING	
SMALLER	θ		

_ · · · _ EFFECT OF INCREASED V_{G2} AT CONSTANT CURRENT

SMALLER	α_1	SMALLER	θ
SMALLER	r_c	SMALLER	r_0
LARGER	α_2	LESS DEFL. DEFOCUSING	

Figure 3.5 Biasing influences on beam formation.

Examples of interplay between the grids are shown in Fig. 3.5. Values not defined are r_O for spot radius at view screen; and r_C for radius at the cathode where the beam is being formed. The example noted for increased E_{VS} (anode voltage) shows smaller theta and alpha angles, which would be counterproductive to increasing image quality at first glance. However, the increase in luminance output may be a higher priority or produce the alternative benefit of reducing beam current for the same luminance output while achieving a smaller pixel.

The third example in the figure, increasing V_{G2} at constant current, looks good for spot size and less deflection defocusing. Again, there are trade-offs that negate positive effects with problem areas. When G_2 is increased, two things change: the cutoff voltage becomes more negative to extinguish the spot, and the mechanical aperture of G_1 appears smaller (to the electrons) owing to the electrical fields. This results in the electron cloud being pulled from a smaller area of the cathode (higher cathode loading) and more drive voltage being required to achieve equal beam current. Long-term problems using this scenario are a shorter cathode life and loss of dynamic range because the video amplifier runs out of response sooner.

3.3 Upper Gun Structure (Lens)

As noted in Section 3.1, there are two basic lens systems in monochrome, the unipotential and the bipotential. Color guns can mimic either the unipotential or bipotential form factor. The performance of any lens is limited by its diameter (i.e., the inside diameter available for the beam to pass through.) The larger the through-clearance, the less lens-induced distortion. The neck tubing (glass) is the confining structure and it is expressed in millimeters (o.d.) at standard sizes of 20 mm, 22 mm, 29 mm, and 36 mm. Small-necked color and monochrome CRTs use 22 mm and 20 mm, respectively. The 22-mm tubing has a thicker glass wall to support the heavier color optics. The net internal clearance is approximately the same as in the 20-mm monochrome CRT. Twenty-nine millimeter tubing is standard for both color and monochrome, while 36 mm is found in high-end monochrome medical-grade displays.

Keeping in mind that high-voltage potentials are part of the upper gun structure in all cases, the need to accelerate the beam and optimize the theta angle without pulling the beam apart (V_r) is the key factor in front of screen performance. The convergence of the beam to a spot, the individual pixel, determines the resultant modulation transfer function (MTF). The 10% rule for beam diameter (through the lens) is predicated on the limits of containment for an energy field. At what point is the attraction of an individual electron asymmetrical enough to impart a radial velocity (V_r)? As shown in Fig. 3.6, the growth in beam diameter increasingly puts more of the beam in an unequal field.

The electrons at the outer edge of the black inner circle are, in relative terms, in a more uniform electrical field than those at the edge of the larger gray beam cross section. Gun biasing selection and higher drive conditions both contribute to the growth of the beam diameter through the lens. Designing a high-resolution display requires all the influencing factors to be considered to avoid inferior performance.

Neck diameter is a limiting factor that will contribute to lower MTFs in the vertical axis of the pixels. A 36-mm neck will start out at a higher performance level than a 29-mm neck with similar optics, provided other aspects of the display system are of equal performance.

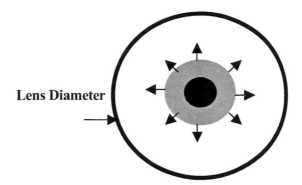

Figure 3.6 The internal through-clearance of a lens element relies on an equal energy field around the beam bundle. The larger the beam diameter, the greater the delta between opposite sides, pulling the electrons outward.

3.4 Cathode Selection

From the very start of its emissive life, the cathode is depleting the available electrons. The drive of the video amplifier does not contribute to the electron flow; it is merely a voltage potential that causes electrons to flow at a specific rate. Barium is the source of electrons in both oxide and dispenser cathodes. The process of giving up electrons leaves behind atoms that are now short of valence electrons. This in turn causes cathode material to migrate to the G_1 area and deposit itself. Over extended operating times, the migrated material changes the electrical biasing characteristics of the optics, which is observed as black-level drift. The remedy is to periodically adjust the brightness to maintain proper settings for the black level.

Cathode aging (or depletion) is a failure mode for all CRT-based displays. There are two basic types of cathode material, with subgroups based on additives (doping) and/or mechanical structure resulting from manufacturing techniques. The types are oxide or dispenser, even though both utilize barium oxide as the primary source of electrons. The full name for the oxide is barium oxide or scandium oxide, where the scandium is a doping on a barium-oxide cathode. Most CRT applications can use either type of oxide cathode and yield a satisfactory life. B&W TV, ASCII terminals, and even projection TVs use oxide cathodes.

Medical-grade displays started out in the early 1990s using barium oxide and then scandium-doped cathodes. However, the high drive levels proved to be too much for certain modalities. The failure is not that the CRT no longer lights up, but that the electronics run out of drive potential and the optics can no longer handle the beam at the higher drives. The loss of image quality is the true failure mode for medical imaging, and the user should define the limits of this loss.

Scandium-oxide cathodes can serve a number of medical imaging requirements. The important factors to be considered are how the display is to be utilized: modality and time-in-service/day. The modality indicates the duty cycle
and peak cathode loading to be expected. The time in service per day determines
the rate of accumulated wear and tear.

If the use of the display is analogous to that of a TV at home with more
time off than on, an oxide cathode would suffice even if loading is occasionally
high. A primary reading room with mixed modalities but 24×7 (24 hours/day
$\times$ 7 days/week) operation should use only a dispenser cathode. Under the latter
conditions, judicious use of screen savers can extend the CRTs life. A simple
rule of thumb for a medical display is that if the specification calls for more
than 136 cd/m^2 (40 fL) on a regular basis, a dispenser cathode should be used.
(Applies to $\geqslant$20-inch CRT.)

3.4.1 Cathode life

For comparison purposes, cathode life has to be determined under life test conditions to be accurate and useful. Applying the results to actual use is a difficult task. The variables are too numerous and impossible to control, so a best
estimate, while arbitrary, is the only recourse. The CRT manufacturer divides
cathode life into two categories, short- and long-term aging. Short-term aging
is generally of little interest unless some break-in period is appropriate; the display manufacturer should deal with this issue if it is present. Long-term aging
represents the cost of ownership under harsh usage 24 hours per day, seven days
a week at normal operating conditions while the display circuits and their technology still have useful life remaining when the cathode is exhausted. The life
charts for short- and long-term properties, shown in Figs. 3.7 and 3.8, were prepared using accelerated aging techniques. This provides quicker results for new
cathodes under test and can be correlated with normal operating conditions.

Accelerated life testing is accomplished by boiling the electrons off at a
faster rate than normal. This is done using an elevated cathode temperature by
increasing the filament voltage 10% above specification. A 12-V dc filament
becomes 13.2-V dc and increases the rate of depletion by approximately 50%.
The actual cathode loading is also put at a higher than normal load for additional
stress. In Fig. 3.7 the operating conditions are noted as $I_C = 400$ µA (cathode
current), $G_2 = 800$ V, and the aperture of G_1 is 0.014 inch. To put this into
perspective with normal conditions, on a 21-inch FS CRT using P104 phosphor,
the continuous luminance over the entire screen would be 613 cd/m^2 (180 fL).
Using P45, the luminance would be 388 cd/m^2 (114 fL). The worst possible
operating conditions would not reach this stress level.

In Fig. 3.7, the dispenser cathode has dropped to 96% from a new emissive
output after 3000 hours (1 year = 8760 hours). The two types of oxide cathodes
have dropped to 65% and 58% from their as-new performance. The standard

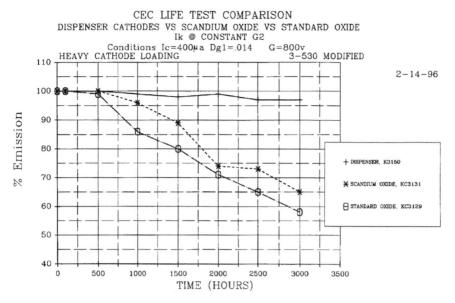

Figure 3.7 Short-term cathode life comparison. (Courtesy of Clinton Electronics Corporation.)

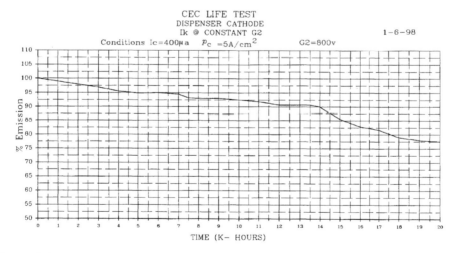

Figure 3.8 Long-term cathode life of dispenser. (Courtesy of Clinton Electronics Corporation.)

oxide goes back to the beginning of television, and the scandium-doped oxide was a product improvement originally developed for color television. Depending on how the comparison is made with the older oxide cathode, the scandium provided an approximately 15% increase in long-term life. Scandium-doped cathodes are more sensitive to the 10% over voltage and have demonstrated additional capacity when tested at normal operating temperatures, i.e., and at 12 V dc.

Long-term aging under the same accelerated testing conditions are shown in Fig. 3.8. The luminance levels would be the same as noted for short-term aging. The oxide cathodes are not carried to the 20,000-hour point. As can be surmised from the short-term chart, their useful life would have already passed. At 20,000 hours, the dispenser is down 23% and there is a knee in the curve at 14,000 hours where the output is down 10%. The depletion rate accelerates at this point for the dispenser represented.

Twenty thousand hours is 2.3 years under extreme conditions. Without correcting back to normal filament voltage, if a duty cycle of 30% of the life test data were used for MRI/CT modalities, the cathode would require 7.6 years to reach 77%. If 60% were a harsh reading room environment, it would take 3.8 years. As noted previously, failure is not a dark screen; rather, when the image is no longer usable as defined by contrast transfer, contrast modulation, or modulation transfer function measurements, that is when the display needs to be retired or refurbished.

3.4.2 Cathode drift

The migration of material with the loss of electrons, as noted in Section 3.4, is important to the proper maintenance of dynamic range. This ongoing process is more likely to be the cause of a calibration error than peak luminance, which changes slowly over time with both cathode and phosphor aging. The cutoff voltage of the electron gun is what is drifting. The black level is actually set to a value that can be seen and measured just above cutoff. The brightness control is the functional description, although the term is misleading for what is does. The brightness control changes the bias on G_2 (acceleration grid), which alters the relationship to G_1 and causes electrons to flow when the video signal is at zero command. The CRT should start from above-ambient conditions, but this is not always practical in high ambient lighting. A display manufacturer has no way of knowing the final disposition of a product and therefore sets black to factory settings, e.g., 1.7 cd/m^2 (0.5 fL) for office environments and 0.17 cd/m^2 to 0.34 cd/m^2 (0.05–0.1 fL) for darker reading rooms. This generally falls along 1k-line displays at the higher black level with 2k-line displays being darker (where black is a measured luminance level). If the brightness is set below ambient lighting conditions, so that diffuse and/or spectral illuminance represents more than the image-commanded values, information will be lost. Although the CRT is being driven, the luminance is being masked by the ambient contribution. Cathode drift causes the same loss of information.

3.4.3 Cathode drive gamma

Cathode gamma follows a power law response. The human visual response is logarithmic and the video amplifier is linear. This combination means that the

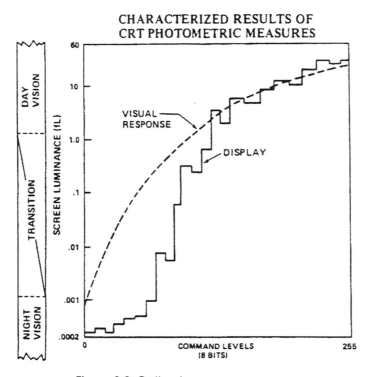

Figure 3.9 Cathode gamma response.

display's natural response is sluggish in the lower gray tones, catches up, and then goes beyond what the eye needs. Figure 3.9[4] is a plot of characteristic results of a CRT photometric response over 8 bits of command. The bit depth is not a factor in this response curve; compliance with DICOM, Part 3.14 GSDF, is covered in Chapter 8.

The initial sluggishness of the cathode-to-command input falls below where black is generally set for both office and reading room environments. This still leaves an area below the visual response curve that needs to be compensated for in either the video card or display video path or both. In the display, this requires a variable gain preamplifier to map the corrective values to the DICOM standard.

Measuring the gamma in terms of photometric response requires indirectly measuring the beam current. Phosphors utilized in medical imaging differ in luminance efficacy and therefore yield a different net result for a given beam current. Beam current is scanned over the active video area and is expressed as current density in microamperes per square centimeter. Therefore, a setup for bias and video amplifier dynamic range that works for one phosphor will not work for another with equal results.

The formula for gamma is Luminance $= KE^\gamma$, where the dimensionless value for gamma changes with biasing. Again, the operating point is located somewhere along the curve shown in Fig. 3.3. The $V_{C/O}$ (volt cutoff) for a CRT

is expressed as a design range. A typical range would be 70 to 110 V of differ-
ential between the cathode and G_1 grid, with G_1 being negative relative to the
cathode (video on cathode). A 70 V cutoff is more efficient than 110 V as measured in volt drive for microamperes produced. The trade-off is a larger beam
through the lens at 70 $V_{C/O}$ for the increased brightness at equal cathode drive.
The 110 $V_{C/O}$ provides a smaller beam at a lower brightness (less beam current) for the same drive. A video amplifier may be able to drive the first cutoff
condition but not the second, leading to inferior pixel formation luminescence
response.

To bias a CRT at 70 $V_{C/O}$, the G_1 need only be −20 V relative to ground and
the video amplifier output held at +50 V to extinguish the beam. For 110 V_{CO},
the G1 could go to −40 V while the video amplifier is raised to +70 V for beam
extinction. The video amplifier must swing from the most positive (off pixel) to
a less positive value (peak luminance) for cathode current to flow, and always
in positive territory. The design approach chosen and components selected in
combination with CRT biasing will alter the observed gamma, resultant image
quality, and the ability to adjust for aging.

3.5 Focus Considerations

The physics of electron optics requires a range of focus voltages to maintain
consistent convergence of the electron beam over the entire screen. The basic
method is to apply a static voltage to focus the beam at screen center and two dynamic components summed with the static. The two dynamic axes correspond
to the vertical and horizontal sweep from which they are derived (i.e., and beam
position on the screen). A high-grade medical CRT that focuses in the center
(static) between 50 and 200 V (a unipotential lens, for example) will require
upward of 800 to 1000 V in the edges and corners. A very dynamic circuit operates in microseconds between 50 and 1000 V peak to peak. The dynamic focus
waveform (scope trace) is a parabolic waveform, which is summed (capacitance
coupled) with the static focus component and applied to the G_4 lens. A display
with digital control can generate the focus waveform digitally with greater flexibility, allowing for differentiation between the top and bottom (of the screen)
and different CRTs, thus imparting intentional distortions to the parabolic waveform to control specific locations. An analog implementation has considerably
more difficulty in distinguishing specific areas. Designs to add a third dynamic
analog axis for corners have been created, but distinguishing the top corner from
a bottom corner is still difficult in the analog world.

What is less known to the user is that the cathode drive voltage also alters
the point of focus and thus the quality of focus. This is caused by the dynamic
relationship between the cathode (video drive) and the G_2 (fixed voltage acceleration grid). As the command level changes (image content), so does the
relationship of the cathode to G_2 and the optimum focus voltage. From just

above black to peak white, the depth of focus (optimum range of focus voltage) could be 50–70 V, depending on the CRT. Depending on where a display manufacturer makes the focus adjustment, the resultant front-of-screen performance will provide optimization at either peak luminance or at a compromise point, all within the accepted focus voltage range for the CRT. Most manufacturers select a point down from peak luminance such as 170 cd/m^2 (50 fL) on a 272 cd/m^2 (80 fL) rated display. While it is harder to focus at maximum drive, there is also little clinical information provided there, so it is better to use a point closer to where most of the useful information is found.

It is not very practical to track the video command level and dynamically adjust focus within the existing dynamic range of focus voltage being applied (based on beam position). This would require delay lines for the video while a sampling circuit analyzed the content. At 5 megapixels it is better to not put parasitic elements into the video path.

The most telling example of this is found with software programs that display text at peak luminance [digital-to-analog converter (DAC) value 255] in menu bar areas adjacent to images. If the CRT is focused at peak luminance to make the text look sharp, the image content will be softer because most of it is below 50% of peak luminance. If this same CRT is focused at 30% of peak luminance, the images will be sharper but the text will be soft on the edges. This is all relative and viewer dependent but easily illustrated with a spot scanner to show how the pixel profile changes with focus adjustment. Since most menus are on the periphery and into the corners, any softness of the text will be noticed immediately at 100% modulation. The corner being the hardest point to focus compounds the problem.

The physical characteristic that changes within the depth of focus is the shape of the pixel column. The narrower this profile, the higher the MTF. The best situation is to have the text at a modest DAC value and have the image be the primary focus objective.

An overfocus condition can be caused by using excessive voltage to squeeze the electron beam into a smaller initial profile. In this case, the brightest 50% of the pixel column is squeezed down, but the bottom 50% ends up flaring outward and reducing contrast modulation owing to added pixel overlap. When properly focused, the pixel column should be a narrow distribution all the way down to the 5% point.

References

1. K. D. Compton, "Electron guns for CRT displays," *Information Display*, **5**(6), pp. 14–18 (1989).
2. K. D. Compton, "Biasing CRT guns," *Information Display*, **8**(1), pp. 20–23 (1992).
3. F. G. Oess, "CRT considerations for raster dot alpha numeric presentations," Clinton Electronics Corporation, Applications Note No. 024.
4. S. J. Briggs, "Softcopy display of electro-optical imagery," *Proceedings of SPIE*, **762**, 158 (1987).

Chapter 4

PHOSPHORS

Phosphors perform the function of converting invisible high-energy particles to lower-energy visible light. The actual mechanism for the transfer of kinetic energy from the electron beam to the phosphor crystal is through the impact of the beam with the crystal. The penetration into the crystal's outer shell of electrons ends with a collision that drives the valence electrons to a higher unstable energy state, i.e., a higher orbit. In a finite amount of time they fall back to their normal or an intermediate state, releasing a photon. The extent they fall back determines the wavelength and thus the emissive color. At 20,000 V of acceleration, the electron beam is traveling at 37% of the speed of light.[1] The electrons' negligible mass is offset by the benefits of the velocity squared, making anode potential a key performance modifier of phosphor luminance output.

Information in this chapter is limited to those phosphors used in medical displays. For further information on phosphors, the Electronic Industries Association (EIA) publication TEP-116C, "Optical Characteristics of Cathode-Ray Tube Screens," should be consulted. Despite the proliferation of television and PC monitors, the amount of phosphors utilized in this way is a fraction of the total phosphor industry. Fluorescent lamps and other commercial devices consume more phosphor.

A commonality of phosphor properties is that they are chemically pure, inorganic, crystalline materials identified chemically by one prominent component such as zinc or cadmium with sulfide. Others are a rare-earth material used in both monochrome and color displays. The phosphors that will be covered are listed in Table 4.1 with both the older EIA JEDEC numbers and the Worldwide Type Designation System (WTDS) administered by EIA.

The first three phosphors noted in Table 4.1 are only for monochrome utilization and P22 is the foundation upon which most of today's RGB color sets are based. The activators influence the crystals not only as a catalyst to enhance overall photon output, but to also target specific wavelengths to obtain the desired color. P45 is a single crystal that can be doped to enhance the red content for photographic applications or shifted more to the blue for medical applications. The zinc sulfide (blue) component of P4 can be changed to yield a bluish-green P31 (GHA) by switching to a copper activator.

PC104 is proprietary to Clinton Electronics Corporation and falls outside of the EIA numbering system. The progenitor of PC104 is P4 from B&W television. P4 has a longer green tail coming from the yellowish-green component that is objectionable on rapidly moving objects; PC104 has a modified yellowish-green component with a shorter green tail. PC104 is the correct terminology in accordance with EIA for P (Clinton) 104. Other house phosphors would have their own letter, such as "X" for Westinghouse or "T" for Thomas Electronics. Over time, P104 has become an accepted generic label and will be used here.

Table 4.1 EIA JEDEC/WTDS Numbering System.

EIA JEDEC Visual Color	EIA WTDS	Components	Dopant or Activator	Component Color
P4 White	WWA	Zinc sulfide Zinc–cadmium sulfide	Silver Silver	Blue Yellow
PC104 White	Custom	Proprietary to Clinton Electronics Corporation	Silver	Derivative of P4
P45 White	WBA	Yttrium oxysulfide	Terbium	Blue-white Rare-earth
P22 RGB colors	XXD	Sulfide/oxysulfide and rare-earth for red	Various	Red, green and blue

4.1 Phosphor Efficacy

Phosphor efficacy is a design issue for the display engineer because once the display monitor is on your desk, it is too late to change the net results. Phosphor efficacy can be stated in two ways, either as a percentage of P4 luminance at equal drive or as current density at a given anode voltage. P4 is the benchmark and represents 100% at a given current density. This provides an easy way of comparing light output deltas in percentages without calculations, and it is accurate in round numbers (delta is shorthand for differences). It is more accurate to use current density and anode voltage because phosphors respond nonlinearly to anode and current changes. A phosphor specification sheet should provide a chart for each modifier. However, as a rule of thumb for estimating luminance deltas for changes in anode voltage, a linear interpretation is quite close.

Table 4.2 compares the monochrome phosphor efficacies along with their color coordinates using the Kelly Chart of Color Designations for Lights, the 1931 CIE system. The phosphor sequence is in the order of least to most blue. A second P45 has been added to designate the difference between the U.S. standard and European standards. The CIE values are sufficiently different for the eye to detect them side by side.

P104/P4 as blended phosphors require the components to be closely matched in performance to avoid color shifts with luminance changes. Just as P4 has a longer green tail than P104 on the decay side, the response time to emit photons plus the sensitivity to current density must be closely matched. Monochrome CRT manufacturing utilizing the sedimentation process requires the particle size of multiple components to be similar in mass so that they settle and adhere uniformly to the faceplate.

The display designer needs to recognize that a video amplifier suitable for P104 may be inadequate for P45. The efficacy difference is significant; the loss

Table 4.2 Chromaticity and light output.

Designation	Chromaticity		Light Output
	X	Y	cd/m² (fL)
P104	0.280	0.304	126.8 (37)
P4	0.268	0.294	119.9 (35)
P45 USA	0.257	0.319	82.2 (24)
P45 Europe	0.247	0.298	78.8 (23)

Light output measured at 1.0 μA/in^2 (0.155 μA/cm^2) at 12 kV anode voltage with 46% transmittance glass at screen center of a 16-cm^2 area. Sweep set to 48 kHz (H) and 60 Hz (V) and 770 active video lines.

of tonal and spatial response using P45 in a circuit designed to just meet specifications with P104 is an easy trap to fall into. The resultant drop in performance can be easily detected with simple test patterns.

The criteria noted in Table 4.2 for operational conditions are not for a typical display. The phosphor data sheets would be a design engineer's primary source for calculating luminance output at operational conditions. However, the quick method is a tool for the nonengineer and will be used here. The first operational item to compensate for is anode voltage. Scaling up from 12 to 25 kV (for a 21-inch FS example) is done by the ratio of 25/12 times the starting luminance output of 82 cd/m^2 (24 fL) for P45 (U.S.), thus yielding 170.8 cd/m^2 (50 fL). The second item is adjusting the glass transmittance at 46% to 50% for the color glass version of the 21-inch FS. This again is a ratio, 50/46 times the results from the anode correction (170.8 cd/m^2), yielding 185.6 cd/m^2.

At 0.155 μA/cm^2 (the current density at the screen as adjusted in the previous paragraph), P45 in a 21-inch FS color glass CRT will yield 185 cd/m^2 ($\sim$55 fL). The cathode load is determined by multiplying the 0.155 μA/cm^2 times 1200 cm^2 of active video for 186 μA of beam current. The CRT specification data sheets would indicate whether this drive current is within limits and what to expect in line width from the electron optics (line width being the vertical dimension of a pixel).

4.1.1 Thermal quenching

A phenomenon called thermal quenching occurs with many blended phosphors, including P104 and P4. Luminance output increases with current density until saturation occurs and heat is generated along with luminance. Increasing current density adds more heat but produces no increase in luminance output. Eventually the phosphor will break down and lose efficacy at lower current densities. For P104/P4, this starts at approximately 280 cd/cm^2 (82 fL), thus setting a limit on the total luminance possible with quality pixel formation. The light output of a monitor is an area brightness measurement that includes all the pixels under the meter (photometric detector) plus reflections within the glass from the surrounding area. Saturation at the subpixel level (individual phosphor grains) goes unnoticed if general-purpose meters are used.

Thermal quenching or saturation is the current density limit that would be observed at the peak of the individual pixel. This phenomenon occurs first at the center of the screen, where the electron beam lands perpendicular to the phosphor. This is where the beam is the most concentrated. As the beam is deflected, it spreads out and reduces the current density at the peak of the pixel. The area brightness remains fairly stable because the metering system is taking an average of all the pixels under the probe.

Achieving more than 340 cd/cm^2 (100 fL) with a blended phosphor requires increased drive so that the pixel's size is increased sufficiently to offset the quenching at the pixel peak. This is counterproductive to generating a quality image.

P45 is not a limiting factor for a display in regard to thermal quenching. It will continue to increase luminance output as beam current is increased and do so beyond the cathode loading limits of most CRTs. Video drive and/or the resultant spot growth at high drive levels typically limit a display's performance when P45 is used.

4.1.2 Decay time

The industry standard is to measure a pulsed pixel's decay time from 100% (initial luminance) to 10%, 1%, and 0.1% in seconds. Efficacy is based on 100%, and flicker (also called ripple ratio) is defined by 1% and 0.1%. For commercial office products operating at 100–120 cd/cm^2 (30–35 fL), a refresh rate of 64 Hz and above will prevent 90% of the population from seeing flicker on a 15-inch display. Since the eye is more sensitive to flicker as luminance and screen size increase (more display area within peripheral vision), a 21-inch FS medical display operating at more than 205 cd/cm^2 (60 fL) requires a higher refresh rate to satisfy the same population of users. Most medical-grade video cards operate at or above 70 Hz on 2- to 5-megapixel displays to minimize flicker. Higher refresh rates would eliminate the most sensitive individuals, but increased refresh rates require higher horizontal scan rates, which reduces the time available to generate each pixel and the ability to achieve a full luminance response.

The decay times shown in Table 4.3 should not be used at face value. The shape of the decay curve and the luminance beyond 0.1% are also important in matching a phosphor to the application. P45 appears to be the longest decay time using standard measurement criteria, but it is the best suited for imaging applications involving motion such as Cath. Labs. It has the least latent image contribution of the three phosphors.

4.2 Phosphor Aging

All phosphors age and this affects service cycles, long-term performance, and image quality over the life of the display. Aging affects not only the efficacy but also the emissive color. Blended phosphors in particular exhibit color shifts with aging as one component's luminance output drops faster in relative terms than the other does. This makes it difficult to change out one unit of four for maintenance after extended use and not see a color difference. Single-crystal phosphors like P45 are more durable in this area. From a designer's perspective, long-term aging must be accommodated with sufficient reserve video drive to maintain the luminance levels of a display while preserving individual pixel performance as much as possible.

In this section the aging characteristics of P104 and P45 will be compared to illustrate aging of blended and single crystals. Aging charts for short- and long-term characteristics are presented separately to show the initial sensitivity versus long term. Aging is measured indirectly using C/cm^2 of charge (C = coulomb = A/sec). By measuring current density over time and tracking it against luminance output, an average performance is established that a CRT manufacturer can provide in the format shown in Fig. 4.1 for short-term aging.[2]

Table 4.3 Phosphor decay times.

Phosphor	100% at cd/m^2 (fL)	10%	1%	0.1%
P4	119.9 (35)	0.060 ms	0.22 ms	1.25 ms
P104	126.8 (37)	0.060 ms	0.65 ms	3.50 ms
P45	82.2 (24)	1.5 ms	2.8 ms	4.25 ms

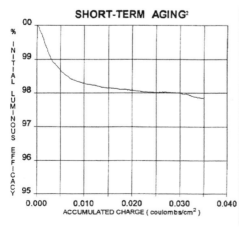 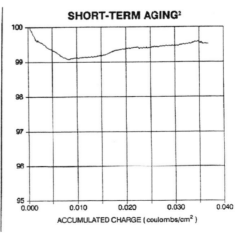

Figure 4.1 Short-term aging for P104 (left) and P45 (right) up to 0.040 C/cm^2. (Courtesy of Clinton Electronics Corporation.)

4.2.1 Short-term aging

Screen burn (also called pattern burn) can occur at any time in a CRT's life cycle when fixed patterns like menu bars remain on the screen, but it can also occur very early in a blended phosphor while a device is brought into service. Short-term aging is something the display manufacturer takes into consideration as part of the manufacturing process. A period of burn-in time is normal to shake out premature failures of component parts; these are the hundreds of passive resisters, capacitors, and solid-state devices that are purchased in bulk untested. Even with board-level diagnostic testing, a few failures will occur when all the boards are connected as a system. During this same time frame, there is an opportunity to pre-age the phosphor.

Using a 21-inch FS CRT operating at a 25 kV anode with an active video area of 1200 cm^2 and luminance of 280 cd/m^2 (82 fL), a P104 phosphor will drop the first 2% in 71.7 hours. This is based on a current density of 0.155 μA/cm^2 accumulating to 0.04 C/cm^2. If the manufacturer increases the current density to 0.2 μA/cm^2, the time is reduced to 55 hours. In either case, the time is too long for manufacturing cycles that typically use a 24-hour burn-in, so a special burn-in program is used to flood the screen at a current density above nominal luminance. This takes a major part of the first 2% off, with the balance coming from setup time and final quality assurance testing.

A P45 phosphor does not drop as much as P104 as shown in Fig. 4.1 at the 0.04 C/cm^2 point. With the same setup as above, 280 cd/m^2, the current density would need to be 0.239 μA/cm^2 to offset the efficacy difference of the phosphor. This would require 46.5 hours to reach 0.04 C/cm^2, which is somewhat easier to achieve. The calculation to determine the above time is straightforward. Divide 0.04 C/cm^2 by 0.155 μA/cm^2 (0.155 $\times$ 10^{-6}A) and convert to hours from seconds (divide the result by 3600).

4.2.2 Long-term aging

The way in which a display is used will influence the rate of accumulated charge; for example, an MRI with slice images on black backgrounds has a very low duty cycle on the CRT and will last longer than a display showing chest x rays 24 $\times$ 7. Long-term aging represents the cost of ownership to the end user in terms of total useful life and how often the unit will require calibration.

In Fig. 4.2, the long-term aging chart shows a dramatic difference between the blended P104 and single-crystal P45 (both short- and long-term charts are included on their respective data sheets). In relative terms, the P104 has a rapid drop to 96–95% from initial luminance output. In combination with short-term aging contributing 2–3% in less than 100 hours at the stated current density, the continuation to the knee of the curve at 96% causes the majority of screen burn complaints with menu bars. Because P104 continues to age at the slope shown, pattern burns can continue to form or can make old ones worse. Pulling

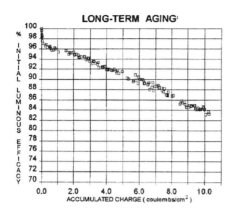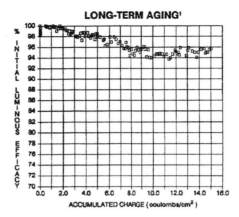

Figure 4.2 Long-term aging of P104 (left) and P45 (right). (Courtesy of Clinton Electronics Corporation.)

a display offline and flooding the screen with a defocused beam can even out early burn patterns, but not totally remove them.

Restated in terms of days, the inset text shows a simple aging situation for both P104 and P45 without compensating for the efficacy changes. In this case, the beam current is held constant over the time period, and each 5% drop is noted in days. Referring back to the slopes of the two phosphors, the P104 would accelerate the aging process after each adjustment because of the increase in beam current to reset luminance to an as-new condition. At the 10-C point, P104 is down 16% and the increase in beam current would be 20% to recover to as-new luminance. The P45 starts out at a higher beam current, but will need only a 6% increase in beam current over the same time period.

With P45, the long-term increases in beam current remain small while those for the P104 accelerate. Eventually the P45 becomes the more efficient phosphor. By using P45, phosphor aging makes a smaller contribution to the end of life cycle.

4.2.3 Color shift

Very few phosphors show little to no color shift with aging. Coulomb charge accumulation is also utilized to measure color shift over time. Blended phosphors tend to show the most change because the components age at different rates. The

> **Long-Term Aging Comparison in Days**
>
> Using a 21-inch FS at 25 kV, active video area of 1200 cm^2 and full screen luminance of 280 cd/m^2 (82 fL) requires a current density of:
>
> With P104: 0.155 $\mu A/cm^2$
> With P45:   0.239 $\mu A/cm^2$
>
> Without adjusting after each drop of 5% in luminance:
>
> P104: 0.8 coulombs $\sim$ 60 days to 95%
>   5.5 coulombs $\sim$ 410 days to 90%
>   9.0 coulombs $\sim$ 672 days to 85%
>   Estimated 1045 days to 80%
>
> P45: 9.0 coulombs $\sim$ 435 days to 95%
>   Off the chart to read 10% drop to 90%

yellowish-green and blue component of P4 will age differently and shift the perceived color away from blue-white to more of a gray. Color shift information is typically available from the CRT manufacturer or the phosphor source.

Replacing one display in a multihead workstation can be difficult when a blended phosphor was selected initially. The color shift and efficacy lost over time will make it impossible to match the color and image quality. One solution is to use a pool of replacements and match hours as closely as possible. The use of P45 will minimize this potential problem area. CRTs using P45 from different sources, JEDEC versus European standard, will also be problematic. When positioned side by side, the eye is sufficiently sensitive to be able to discriminate between the two types.

4.3 Phosphor Spatial Noise

Spatial noise is a change in luminance over a unit of distance that was intended to have a uniform luminance. Blended phosphor by its very nature will have a higher spatial noise as a result of the difference in luminance efficacy between components. As a crystalline structure deposited on the glass surface, the uniformity of the screen in both thickness and average crystal size adds to the noise.

Medical-grade CRTs use finely milled phosphors with grain sizes that will not cause interference with pixel formation. In general, a pixel would need to be smaller than 0.07 mm (0.003 inch) to interact with individual crystals; a 5-megapixel display needs 0.146 mm (0.0057 inch) pixels to fit into the available space as measured at the 50% point, which is sufficiently large to avoid interference.

In Fig. 4.3, a Microvision scan of a single pixel utilizing a blended phosphor (P104) shows the noise content as the difference in luminance output of the two components, measured by a charge-coupled device (CCD) detector. The ragged-edge transition from the dark center to the lighter gray is the difference between the blue and yellowish-green component at 340 cd/m^2 (100 fL) of area brightness. The P45 shows very little of this uneven luminance as a single crystal.

There have been a number of approaches to measuring spatial noise between these two phosphors, with a range of 5 to 15 % as potential answers. The impact of phosphor noise on the image is dependent on the complexity of the image itself. An image with low spatial content is not going to be dramatically influenced by phosphor noise; the phosphor noise is far less than the image's complexity. Complex images with low-contrast tonal changes and sharp-edge transitions in combination with small structures can be within the noise content of the phosphor. A blended phosphor has the potential to mimic a micro fracture in bone or hide a detail. Figure 4.4 shows the noise power spectrum with increasing spatial frequency of an image.[3]

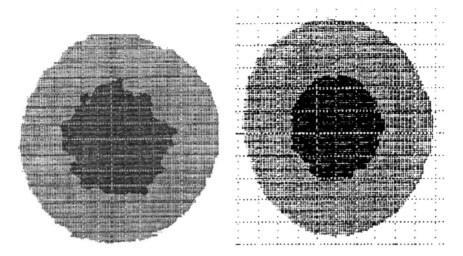

Figure 4.3 Microvision spot of P104 (left) and P45 (right) at 340 cd/m² (100 fL). The dark area represents 100 to 50% of luminance energy, the light gray area from 49 to 5%. (Courtesy of Clinton Electronics Corporation.)

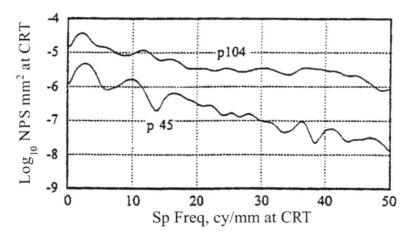

Figure 4.4 Noise power spectrum vs. spatial frequency of P104 and P45.

4.4 Phosphor Screen Weight

Phosphor screen weight is a term found in the CRT manufacturing process to define the grams of phosphor per unit of area adhering to the glass. The screen weight for a 21-inch FS CRT is approximately 6 grams spread over 1200 cm², or 0.005 g/cm². Screen weight influences the image quality and durability of the phosphor screen and the specified screen weight is a compromise of the two factors.

A thin screen is more susceptible to being burned at high drive levels but yields a smaller spot (pixel) than a heavier screen at equal drive. The thicker screen forces luminance energy to move around (scattering light) phosphor crystals that are closer to the glass. The thicker screen is more durable, but the electron beam has a harder time penetrating to the crystals closest to the glass.

The CRT manufacturer's job is to strike a compromise on screen weight to achieve a durable screen that minimizes spot growth. Screen weight will vary over the glass surface owing to the sedimentation process used to make monochrome CRTs. The screen weight can be expected to decrease from the center to the edge. This makes the edge less durable in relative terms, but helps reduce spot size (thinner screen) when the beam-landing angle is contributing to spot growth. The aluminum backing that protects the phosphor is thinner at the edges. This offsets the thinner screen, a process variable that turns out to be advantageous.

Aluminum backing is deposited by vacuum deposition onto the phosphor screen in a monochrome CRT. The phosphor grains are inherently rough and form an uneven surface. To form a smooth surface, water-based lacquer is applied, providing a smooth surface for the aluminum. The lacquer is then baked out along with the water in high-temperature ovens, leaving a smooth aluminum surface adhering to the phosphor.

References

1. P. A. Keller, *Electronic Display Measurements, Concepts, Techniques and Instrumentation*, pp. 91, John Wiley & Sons (1997).
2. Clinton Electronics Corporation, AP (P104) and DA (P45) Phosphor Data Sheets.
3. E. Muka, T. Mertelmeier, R. Slone and E. Senol, "Impact of phosphor luminance noise on the specification of high-resolution CRT displays for medical imaging," *Proceedings of SPIE*, **3031**, 214 (1997).

Chapter 5

GENERATING THE PIXEL

The pixel (picture element) is the building block from which image quality will be derived. A perfect Gaussian-shaped pixel (or spot) is not a realistic expectation for a CRT display. The screen center is the only location where the electron beam is truly perpendicular to the phosphor screen and theoretically capable of providing a Gaussian distribution. Add in veiling glare, halation, and other inherent distortions that make the pixel larger, and the ideal pixel shape becomes awash in unwanted luminance energy. Controlling the formation of the pixel in both the horizontal and vertical dimensions is therefore key to optimizing contrast modulation.

If the electron beam were stationary at the time each pixel was formed, the optics would be the only controlling element of concern. But in a raster-scanned display, the beam is being pulled from the top left corner to the bottom right corner in sequentially scanned lines. The added element of velocity imparts a time domain to controlling the beam current reaching the screen at any given pixel location. As such, the vertical dimension of a pixel is controlled by the optics, but the horizontal width, with the element of time, is controlled by the video amplifier's ability to respond. A slow video amplifier will spread the current out over the available pixel time, reducing the potential contrast modulation with adjacent pixels. Thus, an appropriately matched video amplifier will yield better contrast modulation because more of the beam current (current density) is concentrated at the center of the pixel.

The most inferior display can produce "on" pixels, but may never generate an "off" pixel between two on-pixels at maximum luminance. The display with the superior image quality (i.e., contrast modulation) is the one that can produce the off-pixel in a field of on-pixels by controlling the shape of the individual pixel down to the 5% point of luminance energy.

5.1 The Gaussian Pixel

Figure 5.1 shows the ideal Gaussian profile with the 50% and 5% points identified. The 50% point is the accepted standard in medical imaging and is also referred to as the full width, half maximum (FWHM) point. The 5% point is considered the lowest luminance energy the eye will be influenced by in terms of image quality. A few references have put this as low as 3%.

A pixel can also be specified by CRT manufacturing standards using a metric called the shrinking raster method. This method measures the pixel size at the 60.7% point of luminance energy and yields a smaller number. A rule-of-thumb correction is to multiply the 60.7% value by 1.18 (18% increase) for an approximate correlation to the FWHM point. For medical displays, the 50%

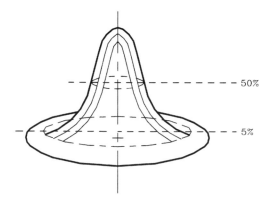

Figure 5.1 Gaussian profile.

and 5% points would be the preferred criteria for evaluation and comparison of vendors.

The drive level at which a pixel is measured must also be specified. Pixel size increases with beam current, so that a specification done at 30% of maximum luminance would be misleading if the optics and/or video amplifier performance were poor above 50% of maximum luminance. The pixel should be specified at 100% and at an average luminance that reflects the CRT's use. This will typically fall between 25 and 50% of maximum luminance. CRT and display manufacturers all use the screen center as the reference location because it gives the undeflected beam performance. However, the quality of the pixel after being deflected should also be taken into consideration. Spot growth is normal and is dependent on the angle through which the beam is bent to reach the edge of the active video. The shape of the pixel is also distorted by the landing angle going away from screen center. The resulting teardrop-shaped tail points toward the edge, contributing to a further reduction in contrast modulation if it is not controlled by dynamic astigmatism. Dynamic astigmatism reshapes the pixel to near round for improved performance away from screen center; it does not reduce spot growth from deflection.

The actual pixel shape (profile) should be a thinned out version of the Gaussian profile in Fig. 5.1. In order to generate an off-pixel between two on pixels, the flare at the base needs to be minimized to reduce the amount of pixel overlap. Pixels that flare out excessively will contribute to the luminance of adjacent pixels; as much as a 6-pixel radius is not uncommon with poor bandwidth.

In Fig. 5.2 a narrow pixel column is attained using 36-mm optics and matching video amplifier with a P45 phosphor driven to 340 cd/m^2 (100 fL). A 2:1 ratio between the 5% and 50% point is achieved in this diagnostic-grade display. Each grid line is 0.001 inch, so that the FWHM is 0.005 inch and the 5% point is 0.010 inch (0.127 mm and 0.254 mm, respectively). The full-screen pixel format is 2048 × 2560 (5 megapixels), which is often referred to as a 2k-line display.

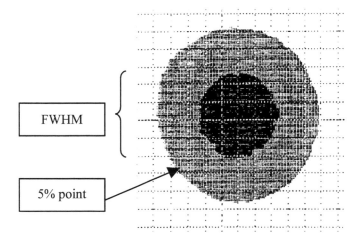

Figure 5.2 Microvision scan of P45 at 100 fL with 36 mm optics. (Courtesy of Clinton Electronics Corporation.)

The same pixel in a 1k-line display would be unacceptable for size and column ratio. The raster lines and individual pixels would be discernable. For a 1k-line pixel density of 1600×1200 or 1280×1024 on the same size CRT, a larger pixel is needed with additional fill so that a continuous unstructured image is presented. In round numbers, the pixel FWHM point would double in size and the ratio could be expanded to 3:1.

5.2 Raster Addressability Ratio (RAR)

RAR is a way of asking, "Does the pixel fit?" In the inset text box, the example for the 1k-line display has an RAR of 0.88, meaning the actual pixel is 88% of the space available as measured at the FWHM point (50% point). The National Information Display Laboratory (NIDL) uses RAR along with a number of other metrics in evaluating performance. Work done by other recognized research centers recommends it for use as a starting point to evaluate medical displays.[1]

Raster Addressability Ratio

The RAR is the ratio of the size of the "actual" pixel (spot or line) produced to the size of the addressable pixel, i.e., space available.

Example: A 21-inch FS CRT has a screen area of 300×400 mm. In landscape orientation, 400 mm of horizontal space provides 0.25 mm (0.0098 inch) of space for 1600 pixels on a 1k-line and 0.156 mm (0.0061 inch) on a 2k-line display at 2560 pixels.

If the 1k-line actual pixel size is 0.22 mm, the RAR equals 0.88 (0.22/0.25). For a 2k-line display with an actual pixel of 0.139 mm, the RAR equals 0.89 (0.139/0.156).

In Ref. 1, an RAR range recommended for medical-grade displays falls between 0.9 and 1.1, meaning the actual pixel is between 90 and 110% of the space available (addressable space).

Commercial graphics and imaging can be used with an RAR value of between 1.2 and 1.3 for a smooth photo-quality appearance. The increase in pixel overlap limits the contrast modulation to approximately a 50% maximum with well-defined pixel columns to as low as 25% with flared pixels. The 0.9 to 1.1 RAR is recommended for medical use to increase the contrast modulation and afford better low-contrast resolution. Lowering the RAR below 0.9 will increase the structured appearance at close viewing distances. This would be objectionable even with the added contrast modulation.

At an RAR of 1.5 and greater, the display will not reproduce the implied addressable format. On a 5-megapixel-rated display, this would mean the optics and video amplifier are capable of resolving only 2 or 3 megapixels.

5.3 Control of the Pixel

As noted in the beginning of this chapter, the electron optics controls the vertical and the video amplifier controls the horizontal dimension of each pixel. The video amplifier (electronic response) also relies on the incoming video source to be faster than the video path inside the display. The conversion from the digital information in the PC or workstation to the analog video takes place at the digital-to-analog-converter (DAC); the term RAMDAC is also used to identify the output stage of a video card incorporating the video random-access memory (RAM) along with the DAC. This output needs to be approximately twice the video rate of the display. Otherwise, the square-wave command pulses desired from the DAC will have a perceived slope and be reflected in the video response.

In Fig. 5.3 the DAC output is a positive square-wave pulse with the peak voltage representing a luminance value. The range of output is from just above zero to 0.714 V. The video amplifier path boosts and inverts this signal so that

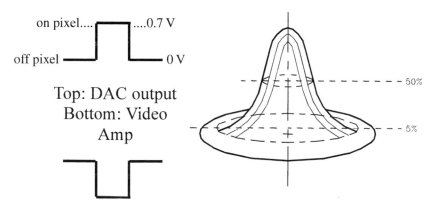

Figure 5.3 DAC output pulse and idealized video response to achieve a Gaussian pixel.

cutoff (off-pixel) is the more positive and a peak luminance command is the least positive, but is not negative.

A quality DAC comes very close to outputting a square wave, which implies that a poor-quality DAC will influence the shape of the pixel as the video amplifier tracks the rise and fall of the video signal, and it does. A poor-quality DAC connected to a quality video path will show the distortion like an oscilloscope would. Saving budget dollars on the video card for a better display does not benefit the image. A DAC that is slowed down to pass agency emission standards will appear to have a slope to the rise and fall time that will be reproduced as wider pixels at the base (5% point), contributing to lower contrast modulation.

The video source and display should be treated as a matched pair. They need to complement each other and not be the source of distortion or filtering of image content. At 5 megapixels the video drive to the cathode of the CRT actually looks more like a sawtooth with virtually no flat area (the top of the square wave) at the Nyquist frequency.

5.3.1 Vertical pixel modulation

The left image of Fig. 5.4[2] illustrates five raster lines in total, three "on" at a DAC value of 255 separated by two "off" pixels. The valleys between the on peaks are as close as this example can achieve in producing an off-pixel.

The vertical direction or height of the pixel, i.e., the raster line, is controlled by the electron optics. The biasing chosen and the drive level all contribute to the net result. In addition, vertical linearity and size will also influence measurements of contrast modulation. Linearity adjusts the line spacing so that squares remain squares from top to bottom. Vertical size controls the dimension over which the information is presented. Expanding the vertical size will open more space between lines and yield higher contrast modulation. This can cause erroneously high values of the MTF for the vertical axis while corrupting the geometric integrity. An example is a 5-megapixel format (a 5:4 aspect ratio)

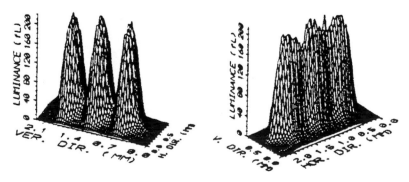

Figure 5.4 Five raster lines (vertical) and five pixels (one horizontal line), three on and two off.

being presented on a 21-inch CRT (a 4:3 aspect ratio) with the image stretched vertically to fill the screen. This will increase the line spacing of the image and yield higher MTF values. The standard 4-megapixel format is a 4:3 aspect ratio and fills the active video area without geometric distortions.

5.3.2 Horizontal pixel modulation

The right-hand image of Fig. 5.4 illustrates five pixels on a single raster line. Again, three are "on" (DAC = 255) with two "off" pixels separating them. The valleys have all but disappeared, indicating poor contrast modulation. Generating an off (black) pixel in this example would be impossible, and low-contrast signals would also be poorly rendered.

Because a raster line has the time domain of writing speed (i.e., a beam sweeping across the screen from left to right), the ability of the video amplifier to transition from one command level to another is the determining factor controlling the pixel's width and profile. Typical MTF values for the horizontal axis are less than the vertical axis for this single reason; the video amplifier tends to be the weakest link in the overall architecture of high-resolution displays.

Pixel formats below 1600×1200 are well supported by commercially available amplifiers as either discrete components (individual parts) or integrated circuit (IC) packages. Above this format, the choices are limited and are typically custom products not manufactured in high volume. An IC implementation will usually outperform discrete components because the compactness of the design offers shorter pathways, which yield higher frequency responses and fewer parasitic distortions.

5.4 Dynamic Response as a System

There are two components to an image, spatial and tonal (contrast differences). Schools of thought support both with equal intensity, claiming that one or the other is the most important attribute of an image. A majority of radiologists consider contrast detail to be more important than spatial response. The failure to render the preferred attribute implies a flawed image. The reality in a CRT-based display is that both elements are inextricably linked to the video bandwidth. Poor bandwidth will cause the loss of both. The one detected first will be determined by how it is measured.

This section focuses on two operating scenarios and the results measured at the individual pixel and Nyquist frequency (one-on-one-off, alternating pixels). Test patterns that reveal a display's performance are covered in Chapter 7. The pixel's vertical axis is included along with the horizontal to illustrate the contribution of the electron optics to normal deflection distortions.

5.4.1 Video amplifier response

The entire stream of video information is represented at the input jacks to the display by a 0.7-V p-p analog signal. Whether accuracy is 6, 8, or 10 bits deep at the DAC, the volts remain the same. The video amplifier path will increase this voltage potential (gain is set by contrast adjustment) so that peak luminance is achieved at approximately 36 to 40 V of drive to the cathode, depending on CRT biasing. The voltage applied to the cathode causes the beam current to flow to the screen that equates to phosphor luminance. (Example: 300 μA of beam current, instantaneously applied to a 21-inch FS with 1200 cm^2 of active video generates a current density of 0.25 $\mu A/cm^2$. At a known anode voltage for a specific phosphor, a predictable luminance can be expected.)

The video amplifier's ability to track the video signal determines how much current reaches the phosphor and how it is distributed within the available pixel space (i.e., addressable pixel). The amplifier's response is expressed in bandwidth as a frequency, but must also include the p-p voltage capacity for it to have meaning. The p-p voltage capacity is stated to a maximum frequency, after which the p-p falls off with increasing frequency. In other words, the amplifier will respond to the higher frequency, but not achieve the p-p output. This is referred to as roll off, and where this occurs will determine what pixel density can be supported without the loss of tonal or spatial integrity.

Figure 5.5 shows a pixel profile at screen center for the horizontal (left image) and vertical (right image) for a 5-megapixel command signal of 340 cd/m^2 (100 fL) as measured on a Microvision, CCD-based, spot scanner. As previously noted in this chapter, the 50% and 5% points are both important to image

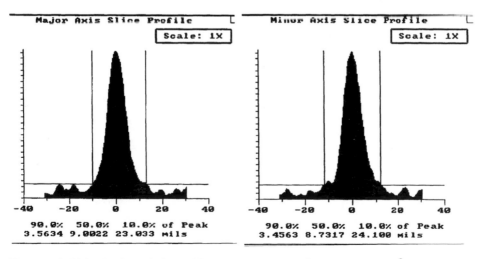

Figure 5.5 200-MHz bandwidth, 29-mm optics, DAC 255 at 340 cd/m^2 command. Major axis = horizontal; minor axis = vertical, at screen center. The orientation of the CRT is not relevant. The major axis is always with the raster lines (horizontal) and the minor axis is always across raster lines (vertical). (Courtesy of Clinton Electronics Corporation.)

quality. The 5% point in this example contained too much noise, so the 10% point has been used for comparison. All dimensional readings are noted in mils (thousandths of an inch).

The 50% points are 0.228 mm (9.00 mils) and 0.220 mm (8.7 mils) for the horizontal and vertical, respectively. The optics shows a slightly better performance at this high drive level. A 5-megapixel format has an addressable pixel space of 0.146 mm (5.7 mils) horizontal and 0.156 mm (6.1 mils) vertical using 300 × 400 mm of video area in a portrait orientation (21-inch FS) and 2048 × 2560 pixel format. The horizontal RAR would be 1.56 at full drive, indicating an inability to resolve the full 5-megapixel format. The current density at the peak of the pixel is not 340 cd/m^2 as commanded. The video amplifier's rise time from off to on is longer than the total available pixel time of 3 ns. The peak is actually between 112 and 120 cd/m^2 (33–35 fL).

Figure 5.6 shows the electron beam after deflection into the upper left corner. Spot growth at the 50% point has increased by a third on the horizontal axis, but of even more concern is the growth at the 10% point. The earlier goal of maintaining the ratio close to 2:1 has been exceeded at both screen center and after deflection. The extra flare down to the 10% point is out to 1.75 mm (69 mils), which indicates large areas of pixel overlap, given the addressable pixel space of 0.146 mm. The values at the 5% point, the desired reference, would be even larger. Note also that the optics shows less growth after deflection using quality high-resolution 29-mm optics.

Figure 5.7 shows the same drive conditions, but with a 330-MHz video amplifier and 36-mm optics. The immediate difference is the narrow pixel column appearance, which is borne out by the 50% and 10% point values of 0.226 mm

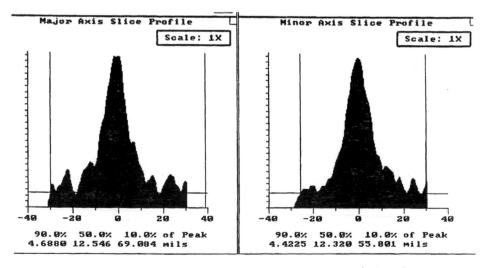

Figure 5.6 200-MHz bandwidth, 29-mm optics, DAC 255 at 340 cd/m^2 command. Major axis = horizontal; minor axis = vertical, upper left corner. (Courtesy of Clinton Electronics Corporation.)

(8.9 mils) and 0.398 mm (15.7 mils) that fall within the 2:1 ratio for the horizontal axis. The vertical axis of the pixel is also within the desired ratio. The luminance achieved at screen center is approximately 272 cd/m^2 (80 fL) due to the higher current density at the peak.

The vertical performance is again superior to the amplifier's horizontal contribution but is also superior to the 29 mm shown in Fig. 5.5 at the lower 120 cd/m^2 achieved. After deflection (refer to Fig. 5.8) the 36-mm optics shows

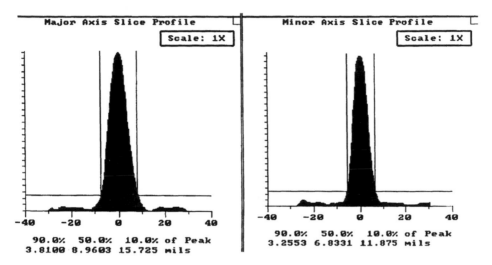

Figure 5.7 330-MHz bandwidth, 36-mm optics, DAC 255 at 340 cd/m^2 command. Major axis = horizontal; minor axis = vertical, screen center. (Courtesy of Clinton Electronics Corporation.)

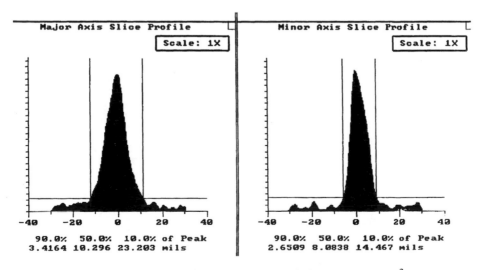

Figure 5.8 330-MHz bandwidth, 36-mm optics, DAC 255 at 340 cd/m^2 command. Major axis = horizontal; minor axis = vertical, upper left corner. (Courtesy of Clinton Electronics Corporation.)

growth but far less than the 29 mm, while maintaining better than a 2:1 ratio. On the horizontal axis, deflection spot growth is less at the 50% point and again holds just outside of the 2:1 ratio at full drive.

The quality of the pixel at screen center should not be compromised because distortions at screen center are compounded by deflection distortion. Based on the 50% points at screen center only, these two examples are not that far apart as they would be specified on a data sheet. Incorporating the 5% point and also delineating the drive level at which the measurements are taken will provide a better benchmark for evaluating and comparing displays.

The shape of the pixel (horizontal) for each of these slice profiles is directly related to the rise and fall time of the video amplifier. The 200-MHz amplifier is unable to concentrate the beam current in the available space within the time available. The loss of current density at the peak of the individual pixel is a loss of tonal accuracy. The overlapping of numerous pixels at the 5% point will be perceived as being an out-of-focus condition when it is actually a loss of spatial response, i.e., sharp edges cannot be rendered.

As best as it can be reproduced in printed form, Fig. 5.9 illustrates the tonal loss at the peak of the isolated pixels and the wider base. The shortfall in current density of monitor B also gives the appearance of darker off-pixels because of the loss in peak luminance. With a medical image on the screen, monitor B could be judged to have the higher contrast, when in reality it is lower. This test pattern uses command values from a Briggs test pattern and presents the pixels between intersecting black lines.

5.4.2 Depth of modulation

Depth of modulation (DMOD) is a display manufacturer's version of modulation transfer function (MTF) that looks at the most extreme operating condition

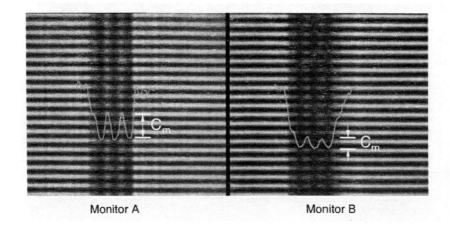

Monitor A   Monitor B

Figure 5.9 Low-contrast pixels isolated by the intersection of black vertical lines. (Courtesy of Aerospace Corporation.)

to find the performance limits of the video path. For any display, this would be alternating on-off-on pixels over the entire screen. From black to peak white (DAC 0 to 255) requires the full bandwidth and p-p volt swing of the amplifier to support the specified pixel density. (Note: there should be additional p-p capacity available to compensate for aging of the CRT.) When this pattern is scanned with a CCD-based device, a surface map of peaks and valleys is rendered that includes all the attributes of the individual pixels plus any negative influences such as veiling glare and excess flare of the 5% point. Depth of modulation is expressed as percent delta between the peaks and valleys.

In Fig. 5.10 the upper scan shows a 55.35% delta for the vertical axis representing lines formed by the 29-mm optics. The lower scan shows a 48.5% delta for the horizontal axis representing vertical lines controlled by the video amplifier. The setup is the same as that used for the individual pixels at 5 megapixels with a DAC of 255 equal to 340 cd/m^2 (100 fL). Again, the peaks are not achieving the command level and the off-pixels between the on-pixels are being filled in with luminance.

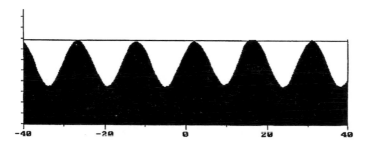

DMOD = 055.35 %

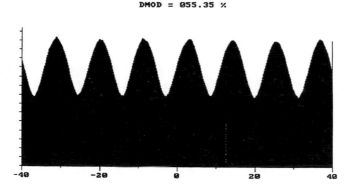

DMOD = 48.5 %

Figure 5.10 DMOD for a 200-MHz amplifier and 29-mm optics at screen center. Top scan is vertical axis; bottom scan is horizontal axis of alternating lines and pixels, respectively. (Courtesy of Clinton Electronics Corporation.)

Figure 5.11 shows the intrinsic influence of deflection into the upper left corner. Again, the optics retain better control over the beam holding the DMOD at 42.8%. The effects of the wide 5% point, which was observed on the individual pixel, is readily apparent in the lower scan at a DMOD of 16.99%.

The drop in DMOD from screen center (48.5%) to the upper left corner is a transition that accelerates with increasing deflection angle of the beam. The screen center and the immediate area defined by a radius of about 6 cm will exhibit DMOD values similar to the center before the change commences in earnest. The peak luminance is reduced, as was noted for the individual pixel, although an area brightness measurement with a meter will not indicate it.

As a worst-case test scenario, the alternating pixels also indicate the maximum response of the video amplifier in conjunction with all other influences. The command signal was zero (DAC 0) to full on (DAC 255) and the video amplifier was only able to achieve 48.5% at screen center and tapered off to 16.99% into the corner. The video amplifier could just as easily have been started at a DAC 50 and commanded to DAC 255 and still not achieve peak luminance.

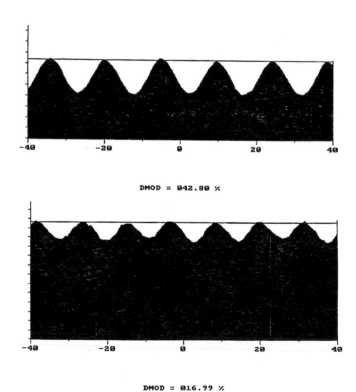

Figure 5.11 DMOD for a 200-MHz amplifier and 29-mm optics in upper left corner. Top scan is vertical axis; bottom scan is horizontal axis of alternating lines and pixels, respectively. (Courtesy of Clinton Electronics Corporation.)

If the pattern of pixels is altered to a large test patch for calibration (~10% of active area), peak luminance would be achieved. Large test patch areas do not place a demand on the video amplifier; the patch represents a static command value at what is referred to as the dc response of the amplifier.

The second example at 330-MHz bandwidth and 36-mm optics will carry the improved pixel performance over into the DMOD results. In Fig. 5.12 the top scan of the vertical axis is 65.47%, reflecting the larger lens diameter over the 29 mm. The bottom scan of the horizontal axis is 67.3%, reflecting the narrower pixel column and 5% point that was within the 2:1 ratio generated by the faster video.

After deflection into the corner as shown in Fig. 5.13, the vertical scan shows 68.29%, which is higher than the center. This is not an anomaly, but the result of dynamic astigmatism maintaining the shape of the pixel closer to round. The bottom scan has dropped to 59.68%, which is higher in the corner than the 200 MHz measured at screen center. The shape of the pixels also confirms that

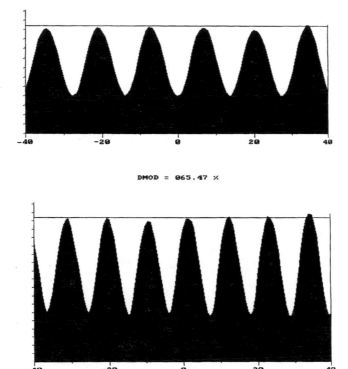

DMOD = 065.47 %

DMOD = 067.30 %

Figure 5.12 DMOD for a 330-MHz amplifier and 36-mm optics at screen center. Top scan is vertical axis; bottom scan is horizontal axis of alternating lines and pixels, respectively. (Courtesy of Clinton Electronics Corporation.)

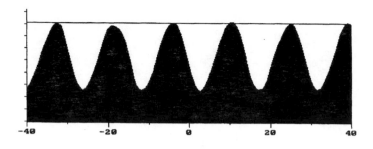

DMOD = 068.29 %

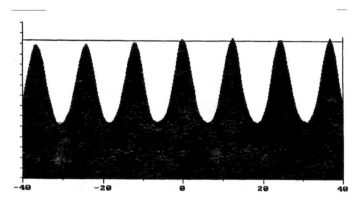

DMOD = 059.68 %

Figure 5.13 DMOD for a 330-MHz amplifier and 36-mm optics in upper left corner. Top scan is vertical axis; bottom scan is horizontal axis of alternating lines and pixels, respectively. (Courtesy of Clinton Electronics Corporation.)

the pixel time available is at the limits of the amplifier; there is little or no dwell time at command level, i.e., the ideal square-wave response ends up as a sawtooth.

5.4.3 Calibration errors

The foregoing examples of performance have a direct impact on achieving and maintaining a calibration standard. Whether it is the DICOM Part 3.14 GSDF or an internal facility procedure, the performance attributes of the 200-MHz example will also corrupt the calibration. The point at which the video amplifier starts to roll off coincides with where image quality starts to drop.

A video amplifier can respond to a dc voltage (a steady-state video signal) and on up to the stated frequency response at a specified peak-to-peak voltage. At higher frequencies the p-p output falls, with a resultant loss of tonal accuracy;

i.e., the amplifier does not achieve the volt drive needed to generate the beam current required for the pixel.

A test patch area in accordance with DICOM equates to the dc response at which a poorly matched video amplifier would still achieve the luminance test points. Only the first pixel at the left edge of the test patch is high frequency to the amplifier because it is a transition point between surround and target command values. Within 5 pixels, the worst amplifier would achieve the command pixel value at a dc state. Not until the beam reaches the right edge of the test patch does another transition occur. Amplifiers ranging in performance from 135 to 330 MHz will all indicate compliance at each luminance level from just above black to peak white on a 2k display, when in reality only the 330-MHz has the performance to track the DICOM GSDF into the higher spatial frequencies and render the tonal values.

Figure 5.14 is intended for illustration purposes only; it is not scaled for interpolation. For the two basic categories of display, 1k and 2k lines, three bandwidth values are noted that cover a range of potential design levels available either as off-the-shelf commercial amplifier packages or custom implementations. The optimum bandwidth will track the human visual system (HVS) response for most of the curve before rolling off at the highest spatial or tonal commands. The midlevel amplifier will roll off at some intermediate point and the low bandwidth will start sooner.

All examples would track the HVS curve at the beginning, where the lines are shown separated for convenience. This is in the dc response range for the

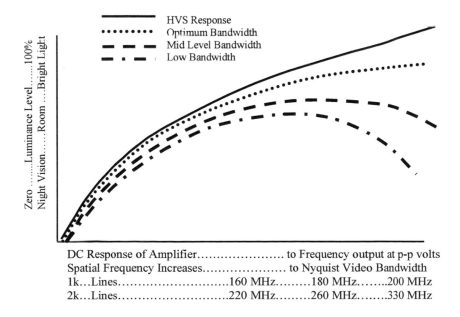

Figure 5.14 DICOM GSDF curve (HVS) in relation to bandwidth rolloff.

amplifier and is where calibration measurements are performed in accordance with DICOM. As image complexity increases (i.e., there is greater spatial content), the need to select the higher bandwidth becomes critical to rendering the image accurately; maintaining the calibration process is critical regardless of the image's complexity.

References

1. E. Muka, K. Kohm, and B. Whiting, "Deploying CRT soft-copy displays in medical imaging systems: A discussion of basic issues," SPIE, 99 Poster Paper.
2. H. Roehrig, T. Ji, H. Blume, "High-resolution, High-brightness CRT display systems: up-date on state of the art," *SID Digest*, **XXV**, pp. 221 (1994).

Chapter 6

LUMINANCE UNIFORMITY

Luminance nonuniformity is present in both hardcopy and softcopy images. A light box with fluorescent lamps has hot spots directly over the lamps when measured with a meter. These are visible as shown in Fig. 6.1. Light is reflected off the interior surfaces to be summed with the photons that exit directly into the platen (diffusing plate). A light box has internal corners and edges in which the ability to maintain uniformity is compromised. For a quality light box, this can be as much as 30% from center to edge. A poorly maintained one can be as high as 50%. The question is whether the nonuniformity can be observed when reading film. It turns out this is difficult to discern and therefore is a minor inconvenience.

The cone of vision defined by the fovea covers a small area of an image at normal reading distance. Within that area, the change in luminance that is due to nonuniformity is minor in relation to image content. You would need to stand back to bring enough area into the fovea to detect the changes with a flat field (uniform luminance); detecting it on film is even harder. Before reading the next paragraph, chose any line of text and focus on the first character of the first word. See how many other words can be read without moving your focus off of the first character; that is the limitation of the fovea and your ability to see details. Nonuniformity on a light box or CRT display has a very low frequency; only a fraction of a cycle is within the CRT's display area, making it difficult at best to detect at normal viewing distances.

CRT-based displays are naturally nonuniform for a number of reasons, some of which have been presented in Chapter 1 and Chapter 2. Other reasons are found in the circuits and how they must operate to avoid other problems. A poor engineering design decision can also lead to nonuniformity from top to bottom as opposed to the expected center-to-edge nonuniformity.

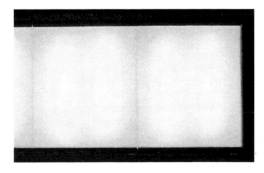

Figure 6.1 View box of typical luminance uniformity.

**LUMINANCE UNIFORMITY OF FLAT SURFACE CRT
WITH PIXEL MATRIX 1200 X 1600 AT COMMAND
LEVEL 256 ADU**

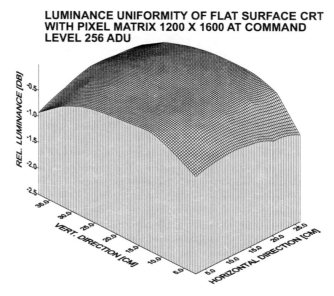

Figure 6.2 (Image courtesy of Hans Roehrig.)

Overall, the glass is the major source of nonuniformity for a CRT. Compensating for just this factor is normally sufficient, although most light boxes can be used without compensation of any kind. (The contribution of color glass with a 21-inch FS bulb is 7% using 55% transmittance. The same bulb in monochrome is just under 15%, which is still half that of a typical light box.) How compensation is effected is important to image quality; it is sometimes better to ignore it for the higher contrast potential. Figure 6.2 illustrates the luminance uniformity of a true flat CRT. This most recent glass design further increases the wedge shape of the faceplate while providing improved ergonomics for the viewer.

6.1 Sweep Circuit Contributions

The electron beam in a CRT starts from the left edge of the video and writes one raster line across the center to the right edge. The distance the beam travels changes from maximum to minimum to maximum again. To the CRT engineer this is the throw distance. Think of the inside radius of a CRT as a circle with a variable radius that the beam is being pulled across. At a constant angular velocity, the beam has a higher linear velocity at the edges than when it transitions through the center. At a constant pixel on time, the pixels are wider at the edge than the center, which also means the current density has been reduced. At screen center the linear velocity is lower, yielding higher current density as less space is traversed.

A display also has specifications for linearity so that circles remain circles and squares are squares; i.e., the geometry has integrity. Each raster line has a fixed amount of time based on the horizontal synchronization pulse

(H-sync) timing. Compensation for geometry requires that the beam-writing speed changes with position so that the net result looks as if there is only one radius and geometry is preserved. The H-sync sweep is typically depicted in illustrations as a linear-ramp sawtooth. It is actually an "S-shaped" ramp, which is defined by a capacitance value in the horizontal circuits; it is referred to as the "S correction." Because the writing speed changes with different pixel formats, a multisync display must be able to select from a range of values. Only the pixel format that falls in the center of each possible available range is optimized for geometry. Formats at the edge of the range are compromised. Industry standard formats are generally designed to fall into the center sweet zone using one fixed value (highest horizontal frequency available) and three selectable capacitance values that can be summed in combination with the fixed value. When all four capacitors are summed together, the lowest frequency (typically SVGA, 800×600) for the display is being corrected.

The sweep circuits, including the vertical, can only be used for geometric integrity. The relationship of writing speed to current density has to be ignored.

6.2 Beam Landing Angle

Beam landing angle was discussed in Chapter 3, and is a significant contributor to pixel deformation and lower current density. As described earlier, the electron beam is a cone (focused to a point) landing perpendicular only at the screen center. As the beam sweeps across the screen away from center, a plane (the faceplate) defines the landing angle as a cross section of the beam. The result is a teardrop-shaped pixel with the narrowest end pointing toward the edge of the screen. This spreads the beam current out and lowers luminance, and the distortion causes added pixel overlap.

Compensation is accomplished using dynamic astigmatism control. This requires magnetic fields to be applied to the beam before it enters the yoke (deflection coils) field. By distorting the beam shape based on beam location, the distortions caused by the yoke are corrected. This does not minimize spot growth from deflection; only the shape is corrected to be as near round as possible. This type of circuitry adds costs, which are difficult to absorb on a lower-cost 1k-line display but are recommended for 2k-lines (5 megapixels). The smaller pixel of a 5-megapixel format benefits from dynamic astigmatism more than a 1k-line display would; it is all relative and the image complexity has a bearing on the decision.

6.3 Focus and Current Density

When an electron beam is focused correctly, current is concentrated at the center of the pixel with minimal flare at the base. A defocused beam makes text look smeared; the edges are blurred or fuzzy because the distribution of beam current looks more like a mushroom cap. A beam can also be overfocused so that the pixel is squeezed down in the upper 50% of luminance but dramatically flares outward in the lower 50%. The text will appear to be sharp, but the contrast modulation has been reduced by the extra pixel overlap. A typical menu bar setup has text presented as either full on or full off (black) characters that provide the maximum tonal contrast with the background. However, the overfocused beam's ability to render low-contrast tonal changes within the image has been reduced by the increased pixel overlap in the lower 50% of luminance energy.

Focus is also a compromise from center to edge. At screen center, the focus can be optimized to the point that no other part of the screen looks acceptable. Digital control of the focus parabola (waveform) provides greater flexibility to adjust specific areas of the screen for best focus compared with an all-analog design. But even with the best compensation, the edges will always be less sharp than the center. The display manufacturer deals with this by softening the center while optimizing the edges as best as possible. As noted in Chapter 3, the less the beam is deflected, the better the focus uniformity; i.e., a 90-deg deflection CRT will always outperform a 110-deg CRT, all else being equal.

Softening the center focus does not in and of itself contribute to luminance uniformity. Like sweep circuits, its primary function is paramount and a minor contribution to nonuniformity.

6.4 High-Voltage Stability

Any fluctuation in high voltage will change the energy of the beam and the resulting luminance. Medical-grade displays are designed specifically for the task and will rarely exhibit enough instability to be perceived. Displays with a commercial lineage that include various screen sizes sharing common electronics are vulnerable. Color displays in particular, because of the higher beam currents, must pump more electrons out of the CRT per frame than a monochrome of the same size.

The typical high-voltage source in color and most monochrome displays is a flyback transformer, which is driven by the horizontal deflection circuit. The transformer's primary windings are charged by the horizontal output as each raster line is written. The beam is turned off (horizontal blanking) when it is returned to the left side, called retrace, to start the next line. At the same time, the primary flyback windings are rapidly collapsed, causing an inductive current in the secondary windings. [The flyback's secondary windings are the source of HV anode potential, high-voltage for the focus circuits, and G_2 bias (first anode).]

If a design for a 15-inch CRT (color or monochrome) is applied to a 21-inch CRT, the capacity of the flyback to absorb the electron flow can be exceeded. The term describing this is called saturation of the flyback. Two things happen when the anode voltage drops: (1) the luminance from the phosphor decreases; (2) because the velocity of the beam is lowered, there is more time for the deflection field to interact and the image becomes larger (the active video area increases).

A simple test program that switches between full fields of off- and on-pixels will reveal video size fluctuations. If the change is obvious at normal viewing distances, the recovery time is taking multiple frames when it should be able to recover within a few. At a 65- to 72-Hz refresh rate, a few frames for recovery would be observed only by a limited population that was also extremely sensitive to flicker.

Displays that experience saturation during horizontal retrace as an accumulative phenomenon with each sequential line written may recover during vertical retrace. Vertical retrace is longer, providing a longer horizontal blanking time to move the beam (yoke magnetic fields) back to the upper left corner to start the next frame. In this case, the luminance measurements would show the upper left corner as the brightest and the lower right as the dimmest. All points in between would follow the sequential scan pattern with decreasing luminance.

The red, green, and blue (P22) phosphors in color displays are not perfectly matched in efficacy. Blue in particular is very inefficient relative to the green. High-voltage fluctuations affect the luminance output and with color the balance is also influenced. This can be measured as a color temperature shift of a white screen or the hue and saturation individually.

6.5 Compensating for Nonuniformity

Compensations for luminance nonuniformity can be implemented from CRT manufacturing to the display control circuits and back into the PC or workstation preprocessing. Regardless of where compensation is effected, the resultant effort should not compromise image quality.

6.5.1 CRT manufacturing process controls

The CRT architecture includes aluminum backing on the phosphor screen for the reasons noted in Chapter 2. Process controls can influence the thickness and distribution of both the phosphor screen and aluminum backing. The sedimentation process for monochrome is naturally thicker in the center than at the edges. Color phosphor is put down as slurry and can be expected to be more uniform. Aluminum is applied under a vacuum by vaporizing a pellet (vacuum deposition); the area closest to the source tends to be thicker than areas farther away. Process procedures and tooling control this disparity for each bulb configuration.

Phosphor distribution does not lend itself well to improving uniformity. The screen weight should be as uniform as possible so that pixel size and screen durability are consistent. The backing's natural thinning away from center actually helps to a small degree. The thinner the backing, the more energy will penetrate to the phosphor. CRT manufacturers have a minimum anode voltage for each design for penetration of the backing. For the large CRTs used in medical displays, this would typically be 12–14 kV of anode potential at screen center (called breakthrough voltage). Any voltage less than that would not produce luminance. Too much thinning of the backing jeopardizes phosphor durability; one of the functions of the aluminum backing is to protect the phosphor from direct electron bombardment.

6.5.2 Variable gain amplifier

This method of compensating for nonuniformity adds complexity directly into the video path. Two approaches are possible: Location specific or a generic model. The first requires the active video area to be mapped for its natural response inclusive of glass wedge shape and beam landing angle for each CRT. A look-up table in the display would then adjust a reference voltage to the preamplifier to control the gain in real time using vertical and horizontal sync information (beam location). The generic model would establish a basic profile of a CRT population and generate a common look-up table.

6.5.3 Raster modulation

This approach applies modulation to the G_2 grid (first accelerator), which is the grid for setting the black level (brightness control). Modulation is controlled using the vertical and/or horizontal sync for beam position and increasing the positive potential on G_2 away from the screen center.

Measuring uniformity under either scenario causes a problem with the metrics. At what luminance level is this tested? A full screen at peak luminance can be controlled within $\pm 5\%$ using a generic model. If the full screen is changed to black, it now appears to taper from black at the screen center to light gray at the top and bottom edges of the video. This would amount to more than $\pm 5\%$ in the lower gray tones as an inverse of the original problem.

6.6 Considerations on Performance

The main consideration when compensating for nonuniformity is to avoid causing the pixels to enlarge and thus decrease contrast modulation. Increasing the beam current, no matter how it is done, causes a larger pixel to form. Coupled with beam landing angle, it is difficult to fight the physics moving away from screen center.

Figure 6.3 illustrates the effects of increasing drive levels to beam size.[1] The CX focus pattern provides horizontal/vertical (C) and diagonal (X) lines, providing a clear distinction between optical and video responses. The pattern is

a

b

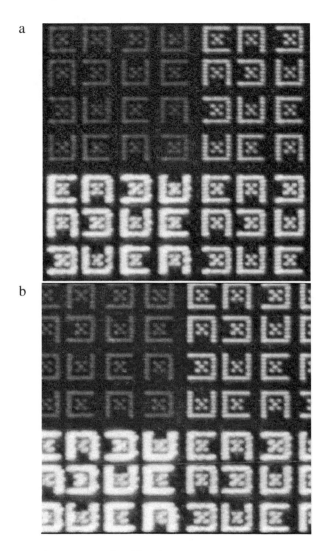

Figure 6.3 Four DAC levels of 63, 127, 191 and 255 clockwise from upper left corner in each example. (a) Max luminance of 220 cd/m² at DAC 255. (b) Max luminance of 350 cd/m² at DAC 255.

displayed at screen center to illustrate spot growth with increasing beam current. The example does not represent the best performance available in 5-megapixel displays, but shows what can occur in what should be a pristine area of the screen. Coupled with the physics of bending the beam into the corners, endeavors to compensate for luminance nonuniformity should be judged against what is lost. A specification driving toward perfection (of uniformity) is going to yield something far less in actual image quality. A specification for a CRT need not be any better than a quality light box, approximately 30% as specified in the AAPM Task Group 18 document.

The video in Fig. 6.3 shows less than adequate bandwidth. The optical contribution, with 36-mm optics, appears to be performing below expectation. At the DAC 255 level, the spot size at 350 cd/m^2 is 35% larger than at 220 cd/m^2. At the Nyquist frequency shown, the MTF is reduced by almost 60%. Nonuniformity compensation would not require this magnitude of drive change, but it is nonetheless detrimental to image quality. At 220 cd/m^2 the RAR $= 1.1$, while at 350 cd/m^2 the RAR $= 1.6$. The display cannot resolve the pixel format claimed.

References

1. E. Muka, T. Mertelmeier, R. Slone, and E. Senol, "Impact of luminance noise on the specification of high-resolution CRT displays for medical imaging," *Proceedings of SPIE*, **3031**, 210–221 (1997).

Chapter 7

TEST PATTERNS AND HOW TO READ THEM

The details of a test pattern can be an excellent substitute for expensive instrumentation for medical facilities. Instrumentation certainly quantifies the performance of a display system in detail, but these are details the display manufacturer should already be cognizant of and have published for reference. Test patterns provide benchmarks that can be correlated to instrumented results and used as go/no-go gauges. A medical facility need only know that a display is not performing; to the extent it is not, let the vendor determine the details.

This chapter focuses on two basic test patterns, that of the Society of Motion Picture and Television Engineers (SMPTE) and the Briggs Test Pattern 4. The Briggs pattern is named for Stewart J. Briggs, Boeing Electronics Company, and will be abbreviated as BTP 4. A number of other patterns have been developed by medical facilities and can be found in SPIE journals. Industry standardization for display interfaces became more organized in 1989 with the establishment of the Video Electronics Standards Association (VESA). A variety of test patterns are available from their web site (see Table 7.1).

The Society for Information Display (SID) is an international organization focusing on the technology of displays. SID members directly and through SID standards subcommittees maintain active participation on a worldwide basis. Their magazine, *Information Display*, provides excellent information on new and emerging technologies.

The American Association of Physicists in Medicine (AAPM), specifically Task Group 18, is completing documentation that may be adapted for medical-grade display specifications. A public document has been released for circulation by the Science Committee of the AAPM. Comprehensive test patterns are now available for 1k-line displays in 8 and 10 bits, along with patterns for 2k-line displays. At this time, it is the author's opinion that it will become a voluntary standard and resource for medical institutions using softcopy displays. Version 9 of the document and test patterns can be downloaded at http://deckard.mc.duke.edu/~SAMei/tg18.

In pointing out specific elements of test patterns, it will be assumed that previous chapters have been read regarding formation of the pixel and the respective contribution of the electron optics and video amplifier bandwidth. Proper setup of a display and gamma correction to a LUT should always be done at installation and then at regular intervals (depending on autoadjustments built into the display). Avoid doing the job twice; verify that proper display calibration procedures have been followed.

Table 7.1 Organizations' web sites.

Organization	Web Site
AAPM	http://www.aapm.org
SID	http://www.sid.org
SMPTE	http://www.smpte.org
VESA	http://www.vesa.org

7.1 The SMPTE Test Pattern

The classic SMPTE pattern for television, a low-resolution device by medical standards, will still provide information on a display's performance as long as the pattern is properly scaled to the pixel format being used. Failure to use proper scaling will yield erroneous results. The VESA web site provides patterns already scaled to industry-standard pixel formats such as SVGA, XGA and SXGA. Adapting a pattern to a high-resolution 2k-line display may require using only a portion of the active video area at a time in order to preserve the pixel and line structure of the pattern. This is especially critical in the horizontal and vertical bars of the SMPTE, which have a definitive pixel/line count. The remainder of the SMPTE pattern can be viewed in relative terms. For evaluating medical displays, use the SMPTE recommended practice RP 133-1986, January 1986 test pattern.

7.1.1 Overview at the macro level

Refer to Fig. 7.1 for a sample SMPTE pattern and the following areas.

Extent. This is the outline border that defines a reference straight edge for geometry. When it is at the edge of the video, the border is controlled by magnets or electronically in the pinning process to attain straight edges. Manufacturers will define straightness in terms of being within the boundaries of a template when projected onto a flat plane. The template will typically have two scribed lines x mm apart that the extent must fall within. A secondary specification for sudden distortions can also be included, expressed as no greater than x mm within x mm of linear distance. An abrupt change in the edge would be called a hook in a corner or an "S" distortion. Gradual transitions that bow outward are called barrels, and those that curve inward are called pin.

Crosshatch (grid). The example has small crosses (+), which are intersections of grid lines not shown. Variations of the pattern will show more complete lines in areas without other details. Within an image, the relationship of grid lines is controlled by the size and linearity adjustments (electronic) and the quality of the yoke. Yokes wound to tight tolerances for winding distribution and designed to compensate for internal compound radii of the specific CRT will exhibit better control of interline distortions. Specifications can be ex-

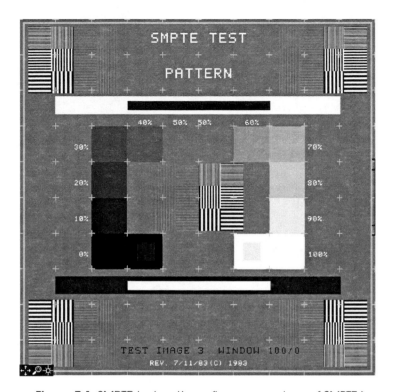

Figure 7.1 SMPTE test pattern. (Image courtesy of SMPTE.)

pressed as percent change between adjacent squares or lines or as a percent of the width or height.

High-frequency stability. Two long horizontal rectangles with a high-frequency edge to the opposite luminance value, the upper being peak white going to a black internal rectangle, and the lower one from black to peak white. The lead-in to the transition point is long so that the video amplifier is stabilized (static state) before a 100% transition is commanded.

One of two bad things can happen to the pixels immediately at the transition: overshoot or undershoot. In an overshoot condition the amplifier goes past the command level and follows a sinusoidal ringing pattern until it damps itself out. This would be observed as variations in luminance of the pixels, and in extreme cases it can look like vertical lines or bars or shadows. It is not as noticeable going into black because one half of the ringing is clipped off, but it is easy to see in the black-to-white transition.

Undershoot is an indication of overdamping in the video circuits. This slows the amplifier response and will appear as a luminance ramp going to the actual command level. This is easier to see in the lower rectangle of Fig. 7.1 going from black to white. The more pixels that are involved in getting to the actual command level, the bigger the problem. No amplifier is going to generate a square-wave response, so one should look for a minimum level of distortion.

Grayscale steps. The pattern of squares surrounding the center in Fig. 7.1 provides a ramp from zero (black) to 100% luminance in incremental 10% steps. Two 50% squares force the pattern to be balanced on the left and right sides of center, providing a full square at 50% in each half. Two additional squares are provided with embedded smaller squares within: 5% within black, 95% within 100%. Balanced performance over the display's full dynamic range would suggest that a difference should be detected between each step, but the eye is not sensitive enough to determine how close it is to being 10% or balanced. The two embedded (5% delta with surround) squares provide a good indication of balanced performance. The 5% within black should be as discernable as the 95% within 100%. A calibrated display will be visible equally at both ends of the spectrum.

None of the areas noted present a challenge to the video amplifier as a true dynamic response with the exception of the high-frequency stability for a single transition. The grayscale steps constitute large enough squares that the video amplifier is operating near its dc (static) level over most of the squares time on.

7.1.2 Details reveal bandwidth

The center of the SMPTE pattern, as shown in Fig. 7.2 will be used to describe the following.

Bar pattern. The alternating bar patterns (sometimes called grills) are paired as vertical and horizontal lines at three specific frequencies. Three sets are at 100% modulation, meaning peak white lines alternating with black off lines and three sets of low-contrast lines expressed as delta percentages of maximum luminance.

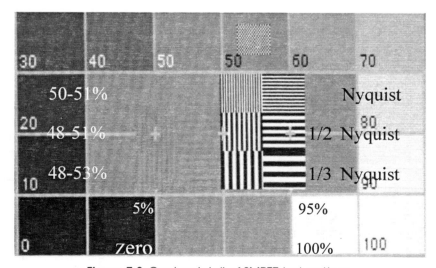

Figure 7.2 Center detail of SMPTE test pattern.

The 100% modulation bars are at 1/3 Nyquist (three-on, three-off), 1/2 Nyquist (two-on, two-off), and Nyquist (one-on, one-off). Failure to properly scale the test pattern to the pixel format so that these bars retain their respective on-off-on pixel sequence will cause misleading results.

Start with the Nyquist frequency and compare the vertical and horizontal bars for focus and separation. The command is for 50/50 distribution of line widths, but with veiling glare and other performance contributions, the balance will be about 60/40 (white/black). Now compare the luminance level of the vertical and horizontals bars. The horizontals are much the same as the grayscale (squares) steps, in that they are at the dc level of video response and should appear to be comparable to the 100% square at the peak of the line (with less area, a line versus a square, they will appear dimmer). The vertical bars require the maximum response from the amplifier since they represent the rise and fall time (~3 ns on a 5-megapixel display). As such, they will appear about 20% dimmer than the horizontal lines, which is what would be expected. Using the grayscale steps for a luminance reference, the extent that the verticals exceed a 20% difference from the horizontals is an indication of video amplifier rolloff. If the delta is about 50%, the amplifier is poorly matched to the pixel format. Correlation would be equivalent to a 200-MHz amplifier being used in a 5-megapixel display with depth of modulation dropping rapidly from the center to the edge of the video as illustrated in Chapter 5. If this relationship is exhibited in the other bars (1/2 and 1/3 Nyquist), then images will be severely compromised.

The low-contrast bars are at the 1/2 Nyquist frequency at the three delta percentages of maximum luminance, as noted in Fig. 7.2. In a simplistic way, this is testing the two least significant bits of eight. Displays that reveal problems with the 100% modulation Nyquist bars may not render the low-contrast bars at all. It is not uncommon for this area to appear the same as the gray surround area or have a texture but no discernable bars even with magnification. On a 5-megapixel display, magnification may be required to see them since they should be approximately 0.28 mm wide (2 pixels) and have minimal tonal difference.

The bar pairs are also repeated in each corner, with the low-contrast bars inboard of the 100% modulation bars. Because of deflection distortion, some loss in performance is to be expected. Problems at screen center are always amplified with deflection; a poor performance at center will deteriorate quickly in the corners.

7.2 Briggs Test Pattern 4

The Briggs test pattern 4 can answer the question of whether the display is truly performing over the full range from cutoff (black) to peak white for both tonal and spatial criteria. The simplicity of the Briggs pattern makes it especially useful for quality assurance testing of installed displays because it takes very little time and requires a minimum of training. Correlation of observers has been shown to be high in the satellite imaging community where displays are tested weekly by intelligence analysts.

The need for a viable phantom for displays is evident; it is necessary to know what one is not going to see before making a read. To this end, the Briggs pattern tests the four least significant bits of eight across the full spectrum of tonal and spatial content; i.e., an electronic phantom for the video card and display combination. If a display is out of adjustment or is incapable of achieving the image fidelity needed, the Briggs pattern will illuminate the problem. Once set up, the Briggs pattern is a quick check on performance that could otherwise slip past the SMPTE pattern.

Scaling is critical to the BTP 4 to obtain an accurate indication of performance. The BTP is 1024 by 1024 pixels in size. Each panel is 128 by 256 pixels with eight panels in each of four quadrants. Each quadrant is 512 by 512 pixels. The whole pattern or one quadrant can be utilized, and if it is expanded to fill the active video area of a 5-megapixel portrait, the pattern error would be $2\times$ or $4\times$, respectively.

7.2.1 Basic panel construct

In Fig. 7.3, each panel contains a series of checkerboards descending in size and composition, starting with B-10 and ending with B-90, the smallest. They are described by the number of pixels per square that define the edge length, such as B-10 having 25 by 25 pixels per square with three squares per dimension, 3×3. As the checkers and checkerboards decrease in size, the bandwidth is being challenged at higher frequencies. Where the video amplifier starts to roll off is the point at which the ability to resolve the checkerboards is adversely affected.

7.2.2 Quadrant construct

The BTP 4 consists of four quadrants, each containing eight panels. The panels are numbered from T-1 to T-8, clockwise from the upper left corner of the respective quadrant as shown in Fig. 7.4. The panels are paired off in descending-ascending order, starting with T-1 (brightest) paired with T-2 (darkest). The next pair is T-5 and T-6 in the opposite corner, followed by T-7 and T-8 and the mid-tones T-3 and T-4. The placement and orientation of the major axes of the panels function to eliminate visual errors.

The quadrant shown is the delta 7 (3 LSB of 8) and the scale below the figure shows the distribution of DAC values for the checkerboards. The T-2 checkers are zero and 7 and for T-1 are 248 and 255, reflecting the 7 digital steps between checker luminance values. The luminance is evenly distributed over the 8 bits. If this were the delta 1 quadrant, the T-2 panel checkers would be 0 and 1 for the LSB of 8.

The surround luminance closely approximates an average of all the checkers within a panel.

B #	Pixels/Sq.	Sq./Dim
10	25	3
15	20	3
20	16	3
25	13	3
30	10	3
35	8	3
40	7	3
45	4	5
50	3	5
55	2	7
60	2	5
65	1	11
70	1	7
75	1	5
80	1	4
85	1	3
90	1	2

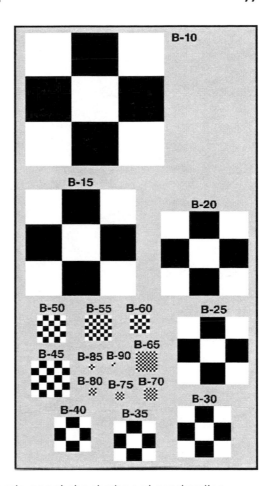

Figure 7.3 Briggs test pattern, basic panel checkerboard construction.

7.2.3 Briggs test pattern scoring

Figure 7.5 illustrates the entire Briggs test pattern as can be best reproduced in printed form. The panel "T" numbering can be sequenced from 1 to 8 within each quadrant or from 1 to 32 covering all four quadrants. The numbering system is used for scoring purposes to maintain correlation between operators. The procedure requires that all panels be scored independently by assigning the "B" number associated with the smallest checkerboard discernable to the unaided eye, i.e., being able to resolve the tonal difference between the checkers. If a display is well balanced across its dynamic range, with equal access to tonal values and the spatial response stops at B-60, the scoring would appear as shown in Fig. 7.6.

For those cases where setup errors are present, such as black-level cutoff, the T-2 panel (darkest) may appear as a solid black rectangle with no checkerboards visible. In this case, the panel would be scored as 2. If the outline of

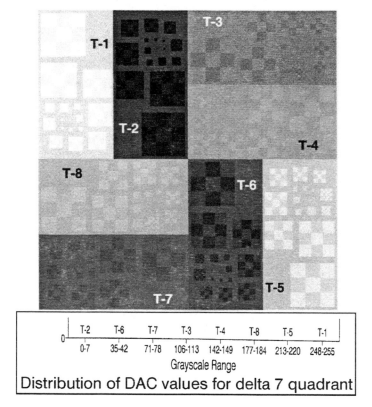

Figure 7.4 Briggs test pattern quadrant. (See Section 7.2.2 for details.)

the checkerboards were visible but not the individual checkers, the panel score would be 4. A brightness adjustment set too high would cause the T-1 panel to wash out and be scored similarly. It is also possible for the T-1 and T-2 (end points of the dynamic range) to be resolved at one B level and the intermediate tonal panels T-3 to T-8 to score lower. A display that is not properly calibrated to the DICOM GSDF curve can cause one or more of the intermediate panels to score lower or higher.

The B score for each panel in a quadrant can be averaged and reported to track long-term performance. As noted previously, all four quadrants should be read to test the responsiveness of the four least significant bits. However, as a quality assurance tool for medical equipment, a single quadrant that closely represents the maximum image complexity encountered may suffice for routine checks.

A benchmark for comparison between displays is that a change of 15 points on a panel represents approximately a doubling of resolution.[1] A difference of this level would be indicative of a color versus monochrome display. A uniform score of B-60 is typical for a quality color display. Referring back to Fig. 7.3, the BTP transitions from 2 pixels per checker edge on B-60 to a single pixel at B-65. Color displays, due to their mask architecture, have great difficulty in

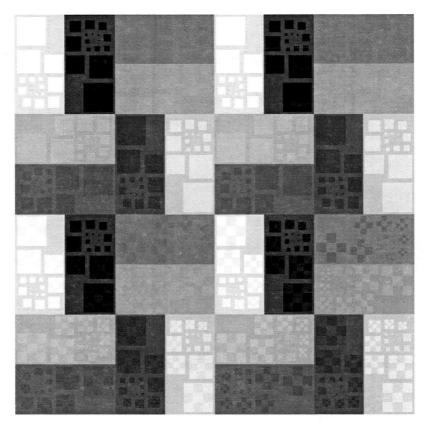

Figure 7.5 Briggs test pattern #4, four quadrants: delta 1 (UL); delta 3 (UR); delta 7 (LL); delta 15 (LR).

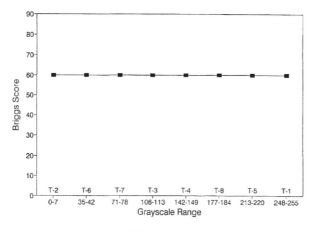

Figure 7.6 BTP score for delta 7.

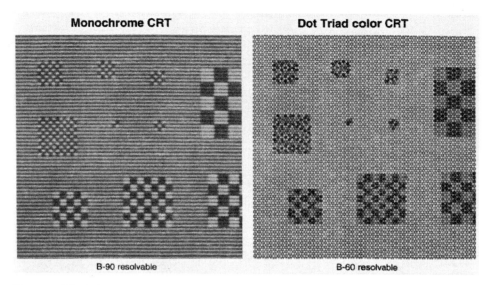

Figure 7.7 Color vs. monochrome rendering of BTP#4. (Image Courtesy of Aerospace Corporation.)

resolving a single pixel, as shown in Fig. 7.7. The B-60 checkerboard is in the lower left corner and B-65 is directly above it. The RGB structure takes on a mosaic pattern, while the monochrome continues to render individual checkers. The monochrome in this example can be resolved to B-90 at a pixel density of 100 dpi. A 100-dpi pixel density format would be 1600×1200 on a 21-inch FS CRT; a 5-megapixel portrait is 173 dpi horizontally and 162 dpi vertically.

Human visual response studies have shown that target size has a dramatic influence on the ability to detect small tonal changes. On a 5-megapixel display that holds to an RAR of 1, the physical pixel is on the order of 0.146 mm (5.75 mils), the approximate limit of unaided acuity. This makes it difficult to see B-90 under the best of circumstances in delta quadrants 1 and 3, but with magnification there should be some discernable tonal change. Again, the display must be calibrated properly to provide a just noticeable difference (JND) between the checkers.

7.3 AAPM Quality Control Test Patterns

The American Association of Physicists in Medicine, Task Group 18 (TG 18) has developed a series of 8- and 10-bit patterns for quality control and evaluation of softcopy displays. Many of the attributes of the SMPTE, Briggs test pattern, and other contrast measurement patterns have been incorporated. In addition, the QC pattern contains a focus Cx pattern in the corners and around the screen center, with the center also containing a series of digitally filtered sets scaled from optimal focus to poor. They are sequentially numbered and would be used as limit criteria for acceptable focus.

The pattern details cannot be properly reproduced within the page format, but a sample is illustrated in the Appendix on a best-effort basis. The patterns are available scaled to 1k-line formats in both 8 and 10 bits per pixel accuracy; the 2k-line is 10 bit accuracy. File formats are TIFF and DICOM, and include two clinical test images. The chairman of TG 18 is Dr. Ehsan Samei, at Duke University. It is a very worthwhile document to have for both CRT and liquid crystal-based display technology.

7.4 Additional Test Patterns

Other test patterns created specifically for display manufacturers would normally be part of a test generator's preset programming or customized and loaded by disk. Medical facilities could find them useful but not easy to implement without a substantial investment in test equipment. A compromise tool from DisplayMate Technologies Corporation runs on a PC using the video drivers present to generate a multitude of test patterns through an easy-to-use graphic user interface (GUI). A number of manufacturers use it for their field service personnel in place of test generators. The program is compact and fits on a 3.5-inch disk, making it possible to install it on most platforms.[2]

An evaluation program from Henry Ford Health Systems was developed to permit single- or dual-head workstations to be tested in situ. A series of test patterns for testing display attributes such as contrast transfer function incorporate adjustable parameters for flexibility. The program is free and is available from Clinton Electronics Corporation on a compact disk (CD).[3]

A 4-Alternative Forced Choice (4-AFC) pattern was developed at the Mayo Clinic with the radiologist in mind.[4] The test images consist of arrays of square targets that vary in size and contrast. The ability of observers to correctly determine the location of each target is used to compute the maximum threshold contrast (MTC) of the display. This corresponds to the contrast required to detect the smallest (1 pixel) target that can be presented.

In practice, an observer is presented with three sets of eight test images. Each image consists of an eight by four array of delimited areas each containing a target in one of four locations as shown in Fig. 7.8. Each image has targets of a fixed size (linear dimensions of 1, 2, 3, 4, 7, 12, 17, and 27 pixels). Each of the eight rows in an image has targets of differing contrast (pixel value difference from the background of 1, 2, 3, 4, 7, 12, 17, and 27). The task is for the observer to record the location of each target. Evaluation of the data results in three estimates of the detection threshold for each target size, based on 50% detection. The logarithm of the detection thresholds versus the logarithm of target size (linear dimension) is fit to a line of slope −1. The ordinate of this line at a unit of target size is defined as the maximum threshold contrast (MTC). The MTC is measured at two background luminances, 15% (pixel DAC value 38)

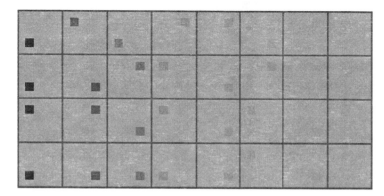

Figure 7.8 The 4-AFC test pattern developed at Mayo Clinic.[4]

and 85% (pixel DAC value 217) as a measure of display quality. The test is time-consuming for quality checks, but would be beneficial as part of an acceptance test on new hardware.

References

1. S. J. Briggs, "Soft copy display of electro-optical imagery," *Proceedings of SPIE*, **762**, 162 (1987).
2. DisplayMate Technologies Corporation, Amherst, NH.
3. Clinton Electronics Corporation, Loves Park, Il.
4. N. J. Hangiandreou, K. A. Fetterly, S. N. Bematz, L. J. Caesar, D. S. Groth, and J. P. Felmlee, "Quantitative evaluation of overall electronic display quality," *J. Digital Imaging*, 11(3), 180–186 (1998).

Chapter 8

VIDEO CARDS AND IMAGE QUALITY

Video cards can be categorized into two main groups, commercial off-the-shelf (COTS) and application-specific (custom) for medical or satellite imaging applications. The latter are high resolution, with precision demands greater than those a store-bought desktop PC can deliver. Precision in this case is the need to deliver truly resolvable pixels and model the behavior of the image path from source to presentation so that it conforms to the way things are seen. Eye response is inherently different from the electronic behavior of video cards and the display monitor combination. In commercial office applications it is of little importance, but for medical and satellite images it can be the difference between seeing something and not seeing it.

Some aspects of COTS and custom cards are the same because of industry standards developed over time, while other aspects of implementation vary. An understanding of the common areas will provide a foundation for understanding the "what" and "why" more precision is sometimes needed.

8.1 Video Card Basics

A COTS color card receives three streams of image data, one for each RGB (red, green, and blue) color, at 8 bits $\times 3$ for a total of 24 bits, which is referred to as truc color providing there is sufficient video memory for the selected pixel density. The RGB information is loaded into their respective video memory channels and then sequenced out to the display with horizontal and vertical timing information. A raster-scanned image is generated by three separate electron beams lighting up the RGB phosphors. The accuracy at 8 bits is 256 steps (0–255), which is converted by a DAC to an analog voltage. The peak-to-peak voltage range is 0.7 V divided by 256 digital steps. The DAC value at 255 (0.7 V) can be 100 cd/m^2 on a 21-inch color display or 340 cd/m^2 on a monochrome medical display, same signal but very different results at the screen. A 10-bit DAC would have 1024 steps (0–1023) available to define the 0.7 V. The implication is greater resolution; however, the least significant bit of 10 cannot be rendered by a display. Ten-bit accuracy does provide a better fit to the DICOM GSDF curve and retention of just noticeable differences.

COTS cards are not considered to have precision DACs nor should they be required to; a desktop PC has no need for them. Differences will abound in COTS card quality, and before one is used for medical imaging, the net image quality should be considered. A quality medical display can be made to look bad if the card output contains noise or has slow conversion speeds (by the DAC), causing distortions to the pixel shape. The same card, however, could be deemed acceptable if it is paired with a display having poor relative response that filters out the noise along with a small amount of image content.

The desired 0.7-V p-p range is not always achieved on COTS or custom cards, and an error of a few millivolts can mean a short fall in luminance that the display must make up for. Changing the gain (contrast adjustment) for the video amplifier corrects this during initial setup. A more subtle issue is defining zero, i.e., black. Since a video amplifier does not like zero because it represents noise, black is established just above zero at 0.014 V so that peak is 0.714 V. This offset from zero is called the black pedestal and it can be anywhere within the first 0.014 V. Not all COTS cards provide a black pedestal, making it more difficult to be consistent among displays. The pedestal also provides calibration leeway between the card and display to define black. A black equal to zero (volts) on the card initially would prohibit a minus tolerance adjustment later. Video DACs are not designed to go negative and the display can do nothing with it.

The level of DAC precision must also be considered within the overall range. Tolerance buildup can alter what DAC 100 represents on one card to DAC 95 on another. A five-step difference at the lower tonal values could be significant, but is probably not noticeable closer to peak luminance. Medical-grade cards use precision DACs with additional attention applied to shielding. This is done to preserve the critical rise and fall times of the DAC output. Shielding also extends to the video cable design, employing coaxial within the cable to protect the signal from outside interference and to block radiated energy per Federal Communications Commission (FCC) rules. Standard VGA cables have less shielding and will use certain ferrites to damp out high-frequency radiation. If the cable looks like a snake that has swallowed something, it has a ferrite bead (also called a core) that adds inductance to cancel out unwanted radiated energy. The higher the frequency content of the video signal (i.e., the image content contains high-frequency transitions), the greater the need for quality shielding.

Efforts to meet FCC rules on emissions can also employ clamping of the output signal, which attenuates the output frequency. This slowing of the DAC response will distort the pixel, with a resultant degradation of the modulation transfer function (MTF) at the display. The application, the image modality, will ultimately determine whether a COTS card has acceptable image performance in the user's eye. Ultrasound (US) and nuclear medicine (NM) applications work well with COTS cards and have no performance requirements not served by them already; US is well served at 6 bits of accuracy. The low signal-to-noise ratio of US is improved by clipping the least 2 of 8 bits. Acting like a digital filter, a slow-responding card and COTS display cannot reproduce the noise of an image and thereby clean it up. The more complex the images, the more it is necessary to evaluate what can and cannot be seen.

Medical cards add a distinctive capability for compliance with DICOM standard Part 3.14, the grayscale standard display function. They provide a means by which the tonal response of the display system can be increased or attenuated as needed to match the human visual system response. This function resides in the look-up table and is also referred to as the gamma correction. The GSDF is the currently accepted standard for the calibration model; the progenitor of the GSDF was the Barton model. Some COTS cards have a gamma correction capability that will adjust the RGB responses, but keep in mind that the primary intent here is to match colors with a printer and it is 8 bits. Some medical-grade cards also provide window and level (W/L) functions in hardware; the alternative would be to use preprocessing in software before the video card. Most PACS and image viewer packages incorporate W/L functions. A medical-grade card's LUT is the best location for DICOM calibration (gamma correction).

8.2 Eight-Bit versus Ten-Bit Internal

The computer or workstation processes information in 8-bit words, and image data are no different. Higher levels of precision above 8 bits are achieved using multiple bytes per pixel. Internally, a commercial card will assign 1 byte for each pixel in monochrome or one each for the red, green, and blue channels. The 0–255 (256 steps) incremental steps the DAC can use to define an analog voltage (video signal) are as close to linear as the quality of the card provides. Each DAC step represents one part in 256 of 0.7-V p-p video output (2.73 mV out of 700 mV). A medical-grade card will expand the 8-bit information internally to 10 bits and provide one part in 1024, i.e., quadrupling the number of steps available to define the GSDF, and fit the image presentation values to the digital driving levels (DDL) required. Refer to Section 8.5.2 for additional details.

An 8-bit in-and-out COTS card provides 256 steps, but the eye cannot distinguish a tonal change for many of them at the display. That means that although the 256 steps are being output to the display, the viewer does not see 256 grayscale steps (JNDs) even if the display can render them. In round numbers, approximately 50% (128) of the steps available are used to define the first 20% of luminance range when calibrated to the DICOM GSDF. In other words, a number of DAC steps are skipped over so that a tonal step is perceived as a JND on the display. This reduces the actual number of grayscales available on an 8-bit card to about 200 or less. In the absence of calibration, using non-precision DACs, and displays with a limited response, the number of perceived grayscale steps can be lower.

To preserve 256 grayscale steps with an 8-bit output, a larger internal scale is required so that a smooth 8-bit output is preserved. For this reason, medical cards operate at 10 bits internally and scale the output to 8 bits, preserving the full 256 grayscale steps. Another approach is to remain at 10 bits for the output stage of the DAC. This will provide 1024 possible steps, but keep in mind that the DAC's range is still 0.7 V p-p, making the least significant bit equal to 0.68 mV, about 0.27 cd/m^2 out of 275 cd/m^2. This is not even perceptible over most of the dynamic range, assuming the display could render it. A comparable example is the low-contrast bar patterns on an SMPTE pattern at 1%, 3%, and 5% deltas of maximum luminance with 50% of maximum luminance being the midpoint. A 1% delta equals 2.75 cd/m^2 out of 275 cd/m^2, a tonal transition just visible on a 1k-line display at one half the Nyquist frequency and difficult to see on a 2k-line display. A 10-bit DAC (output) is therefore of little value, given the luminance the two least significant bits represent. It would provide the potential to render 9 bits of grayscale when paired with a high-performance display.

8.3 Pixel Formats Supported

Using a COTS card automatically eliminates pixel densities for 2k- and 2.5k-line displays, both portrait and landscape. There are gaming and fast 3D cards coming onto the market that support 2k pixels horizontally and more than 1500 lines in landscape mode, but do not support portrait orientation. The 1k-line format is well represented by COTS cards, which support color primarily but can also drive a monochrome display using the green output. After-market COTS cards and video chip sets on PC motherboards have gotten to the point where performance differences are of little consequence and in some cases they are manufactured by the same firm. Larger video memory options are available on COTS cards (after-market cards) that can deal with large medical images. Integrated video chip sets generally follow the minimalist trend and/or rely on shared memory. If you don't like waiting for an image to appear, you should test the configuration first.

COTS cards in general will support all recognized video formats with one or more refresh rates. A card's performance, however, can deteriorate with increased vertical refresh. A higher vertical rate requires a higher horizontal rate. The DAC's conversion rate, the time available per pixel, decreases and it may not provide as clean a signal. The beam writing speed also increases on the display, reducing the individual pixel time and potential current density (luminance). Together, this can contribute to a loss in luminance output and image quality. Displays have an optimum operating point that balances pixel quality and luminance output; the video card format and thus the performance chosen should complement the selection.

Standard formats recognized are shown in Table 8.1. As noted earlier, multiple refresh rates for one format are typical at or below 2 megapixels. Multisync displays operate within ranges to cover the specified total range. If image quality on a display appears weak at one refresh rate, try both higher and lower alternatives. What may appear as a soft focus at 72 Hz may look better at 75 Hz because of the way the display scales between overlapping ranges or the card's output quality.

Table 8.1 Industry-standard formats defined by VESA. Most are 4:3 aspect ratios and fit the CRT active video area without imposing geometric distortions.

Identifier	Format
SVGA	800 × 600
XGA	1024 × 768
SXGA	1280 × 1024
UXGA	1600 × 1200 (or 1280)
QXGA	2048 × 1536
QSXGA	2560 × 2048

The ability to quickly magnify a region of interest (ROI) from a large native image file onto two 1k-line or 2k-line (5-megapixel) displays is unique to medical cards. A medical card would accelerate this in hardware, taking the burden off the processor for greater efficiency. This requires custom silicon, which is not likely to be found on COTS cards. But what can be put into silicon can also be accomplished in software using processor resources. Front-end manipulations of images to the GSDF are available for use with COTS video cards. The speed at which images are presented and the viewing features available are a separate issue the user needs to consider when deciding which path to take. Window and leveling also fall into either hardware or software implementation.

8.4 Connections

Connecting a COTS card and color display is straightforward with the standard D-sub, 15-pin high-density VGA connector. The RGB and sync (vertical and horizontal) signals along with the ground and VESA handshake (plug and play) connections all terminate on pins within a single connector. Most medical-grade displays utilize BNC connectors for video and separate sync, which provide better shielding and isolation. Video to a monochrome medical display is one signal, not three separate RGB colors. In using a COTS card, only the green signal is used because this represents the luminance value, leaving the red and blue unused. Many color displays will also accept BNC connectors, so cables are available. When using a monochrome display and the R/B signals are unterminated, i.e., not connected, interference is possible. All video connections have a fixed impedance to ground. Some COTS cards do provide a software selection to turn off the R/B DACs to prevent noise interference. If not, and temporal noise is observed on the display, terminate the unused R/B connectors (applicable to a 5-BNC cable only) to ground using 75 Ω termination plugs. The noise should disappear.

Medical 1k cards avoid this issue by remapping the R/B values into the green video output, providing some tonal value for Windows icons and applications with color information (pseudocolor). An alternative provided by one display vendor maps the RGB color signals to a composite video within the display itself. In this configuration the RGB signals are proportionately summed at approximately the same percentage as a color display would be driven to yield grayscale. The integrity of the RGB output is preserved and the image benefits from the monochrome presentation.

The standard cabling system for displays operating above 2 megapixels is to have separate connections for video and sync. The higher frequencies associated with 4- and 5-megapixel displays require high-quality shielding to protect the signal integrity from outside interference.

As liquid crystal displays have become a larger factor in the desktop display market, a new series of connectors has been developed under VESA to address the need to connect flat panels as analog or longer term as direct digital. Many graphic card manufacturers have moved to a 60-pin (4 rows of 15 pins) connector that contains digital and analog signals. The cable selected then determines the connectivity. The display end can be the standard 15-pin high-density VGA to a CRT-based display or a flat panel. A digital visual interface (DVI) connector comes in two types, a "−D" and an "−I" version for pure digital and mixed analog and digital, respectively. The −D has three rows of 8 pins for 24 total, while the −I has the 24 plus 5 that look like a plus sign with a pin in each quadrant totaling 29. The last five compose the analog signal path. The DVI-I connector can be found on flat panels with the ability to accept both digital and analog signals. For medical purposes, the digital signal is preferred for flat panels. This avoids an analog-to-digital conversion within the panel, which can cause edge distortion in text and/or contouring.

8.5 Calibration of Display and Card

Visual impressions of an image differ depending on the modality in use. As noted earlier, ultrasound is well served by COTS cards and color displays. The structural details are low and intrinsically noisy relative to other modalities. What is masked by US can be a problem elsewhere. An example would be a structured tonal appearance of a large area with what should be only smooth minor tonal transitions. Eight bits in and out can induce contouring patterns of tonal steps that should be smooth transitions. This can be tested using a grayscale test pattern that ramps from black to peak white incrementally (1 out of 256/step). A DAC that lacks precision across the full range will generate stair steps as interpolation becomes rounding off. This is more pronounced when calibrated to the DICOM GSDF using 8 bits and forcing 256 steps, which causes multiple luminance values to be represented by the same digital driving level.

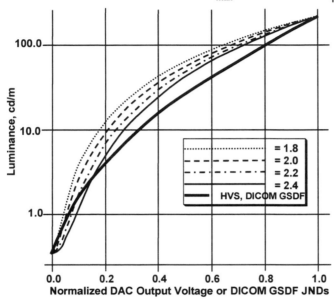

Comparison of Display Functions:
DICOM Grayscale Std. Disp. Function (GSDF) vs. CRT Soft-copy Display
Operating over Suggested Luminance Range: $L_{max} = 220$ cd/m, LDR = $\log_{10}(630) = 2.80$

Figure 8.1 DICOM GSDF versus CRT output.

As image complexity increases, the importance of the video card response, be it DAC speed and precision, shielding or the ability to model the HVS also increases in importance. Whether image quality is being maintained on multihead displays in reading rooms or just single-head workstations for teleconferencing, the ability to calibrate and maintain consistent image quality in accordance with DICOM standards should be routine.

Achieving a luminance result on the display that tracks with the human visual system response (DICOM GSDF) requires a corrective process that varies with each display's natural response, which is part of the design and physics of a CRT. Figure 8.1 illustrates four possible gamma curves along with the GSDF.[1] The natural gamma of the display can be lower or higher than the values illustrated, altering the degree of correction required.

To establish a gamma correction, a closed-loop feedback setup is required so that a known command level is associated with a measured luminance output on the display. The HVS response target dictates the corrective enhancement or attenuation required to bring the system response into compliance. The LUT can be implemented in software or imported to a hardware LUT.

8.5.1 Preprocessing in software

When using a COTS video card with 8-bits internal and no LUT, the means of correction falls to the PC or workstation processor to manipulate the image data before it is streamed into the video card channel(s). The calibration process builds a look-up table representing the corrections necessary. The image data are compensated and then sent to the video card (chip set) without further changes. Each new image coming to the PC would be modified. Depending on the amount of memory space allocated, this would impinge on the overall resources available to the processor.

The downside of this approach is that the output of the video card is not an 8-bit output scaled from 10 bits. The 256 digital steps available are correlated to the LUT to fit the curve and some of the steps will be omitted to achieve a just noticeable difference. A plot of the luminance response would indicate some stair steps bracketing the desired GSDF curve. Forcing 256 JNDs from 8 bits leads to larger stair steps because one DAC step ends up defining two intended JND luminance levels.

8.5.2 Processing in hardware

This approach requires custom silicon on the video card to provide the LUT function so that incoming image data are automatically scaled to the required calibration. As in preprocessing, a closed-loop feedback calibration is needed to establish the corrective values. The familiar handheld light meter connected to the video card performs this function. Resource allocation is improved for the processor because all images are automatically corrected in real time by the graphics card.

Medical-grade cards without exception also utilize at least 10-bit internal image processing. This provides for a smooth 8- or 10-bit output at the DAC, preserving a minimum of 256 grayscale steps. This is illustrated in Fig. 8.2 with the dot sequences (three each) marked as A and B. Sequence "A" is 8 bits in and out, "B" is 8 bits out scaled from 10 bits. The luminance values on the x-axis are in candelas per square meter and at the low end of the spectrum on either side of 1. Default luminance is the natural response of the display to the DAC steps. The middle row shows linearized luminance steps. The top sequence is the desired luminance, i.e., the desired image values for calibrated JNDs.

Looking at default sequence A, you will notice that a number of the brown dots do not align with the turquoise linearized dots. These dots (DAC steps) are the ones being skipped over so that a luminance change is perceived. Keeping in mind that the turquoise dots represent the closest fit to the linearized curve possible from 8 bits, the desired luminance, the yellow dots, align well in some places and not in others. In some cases one turquoise dot will be representing two yellow dots. The end result is a stair step appearance to tonal transitions.

In sequence B, a very different appearance is noted. With 1024 default steps, the ability to closely match up with the linearized luminance steps provides a truer alignment with the desired luminance. The net result is a smoother fit to

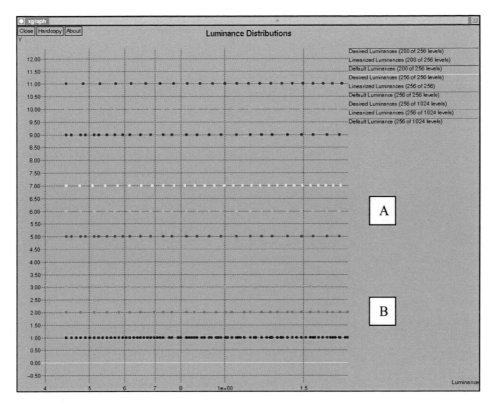

Figure 8.2 Luminance distribution at CRT. (Courtesy of University of North Carolina, Chapel Hill, Brad Hemminger.)

the GSDF curve and greater accuracy of the presentation. The stair stepping pattern is illustrated in Fig. 8.3 with an expanded inset to the full graph. The green line is mostly hidden behind the yellow line until it is magnified in the inset. Here the yellow line with 8-bit in-and-out architecture reveals the stepped response after calibration. The green line, using 10 bits internal, is now more visible and presents a smoother appearance.

A 10-bit output taken from 10 bits internal or scaled from a higher number of bits would smooth the curve further, but the ability to render finer steps is questionable. The impact at the display would be negligible for the best-performing displays given the current architecture for video signals, i.e., the limitation of 0.7 V p-p. Realistically, for a CRT-based display, 9 bits of accuracy at the display screen should satisfy the most demanding users for grayscale rendering, closely matching the grayscale steps that are perceptible by the eye.

8.5.3 Monochrome alternative with a color card

A monochrome display utilizes only the green output from a color card on a typical system. If the card has a software switch to turn off the RB output and map

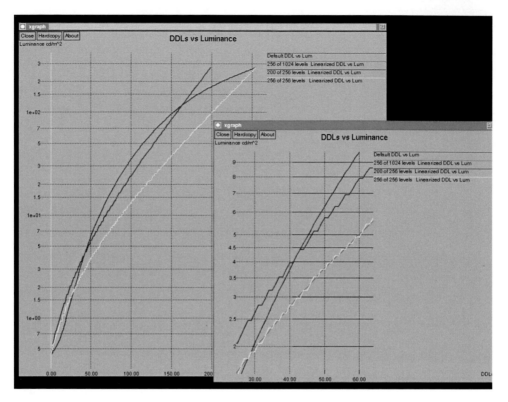

Figure 8.3 Digital driving levels versus luminance output. (Courtesy of Brad Hemminger, University of North Carolina, Chapel Hill.)

those values into the green, the color icon tones will benefit from the pseudo-color. The better medical-grade cards that support color include this feature, but not all COTS cards do so. However, even a low-cost COTS card can provide an alternative on a budget. A COTS color card, when coupled with a display that can combine the RGB in fixed proportions of 30%, 60%, and 10%, respectively, permits a software solution to be applied to calibration.[2]

The red and green channel comprises 90% of the total signal as combined at the display and would function in a natural response mode; no compensation would be applied. The remaining blue channel would contain a parabolic waveform correction utilizing all 8 bits, which would represent 10% of the total signal when combined within the display. In a very simplistic description, at the lowest gray tones the blue channel would be at maximum and decrease to zero at about DAC 145 and then increase back to maximum to the brightest tones. If this corrected signal is applied to a color display with a grayscale test pattern, the color would go from blue to yellow (green and red only) to white.

Provided the display consistently mixed the signals, a fixed correction scenario could be used to approximate the DICOM GSDF and be quite close. A simple calibration program could also be utilized with a light meter feedback loop to customize the parabolic correction. The combination of the three channels would have a bit accuracy equivalent to 10–11 bits, providing a smooth fit to the DICOM GSDF. The original work covered by Ref. 2 (an SPIE poster paper) indicated that the accuracy of the contrast was observed to fall within a few percent of that prescribed by the DICOM grayscale standard. This approach would be independent of the video card, making it possible for a broad population of cards or chip sets to be useful.

References

1. E. Muka, T. Mertelmeier, R Slone, and E. Senol, "Impact of luminance noise on the specification of high-resolution CRT displays for medical imaging," *Proceedings of SPIE*, **3031**, 210–221 (1997).
2. M. Flynn, A. Badano, K. Compton, "Luminance response calibration using multiple display channels," *Proceedings of SPIE*, **4319**, pp. 654–659 (2001).

Chapter 9

WINDOW AND LEVEL

Not to be confused with contrast and brightness, window and level provide a tool to select a range of tonal information from within the total image and present it on the display using the display's full tonal range as calibrated. Brightness and contrast appear to influence the same attributes of an image, and that makes them appear functionally equal. That is roughly where any similarity ends and the need to understand what is different begins. The two sides of this process can be separated at the DAC conversion on the video graphic card. PreDAC is completely digital and where the native image is manipulated, and post-DAC is the analog video signal to the display. The former permits the selection of a range (window and level) of tonal information to be presented while the latter is for setting the display's dynamic response from black to peak white, i.e., operational settings (brightness and contrast) that are to be maintained to a specification.

9.1 Brightness and Contrast Review

Post-DAC is unfortunately saddled with terminology from the days of television. Brightness and contrast are only half correct. Brightness controls a bias voltage to the electron optics that adjusts the point at which electrons will start to flow to the screen when the video is at zero (black) drive level. This would more correctly be called the black level control because this control should not be used to achieve peak brightness. Contrast is like the volume control on a stereo; the user sets the gain of the video amplifier to achieve the desired *peak* brightness, correctly called luminance. The wider the dynamic range desired, the more gain (bandwidth response) required. If black is defined as 1.7 cd/m^2 (0.5 fL) and peak luminance at 272 cd/m^2 (80 fL), the amplifier gain (contrast control) is set to deliver a peak-to-peak swing of 270.3 cd/m^2. If the peak needs to be 340 cd/m^2 (100 fL), there had better be some more gain left in the amplifier. When the amplifier reaches its bandwidth limit, the only way left to achieve peak is to raise the black level. This only appears to help by shifting the luminance range upward, with the loss of the darker gray tones. Internally, the electron optics does have limits of drive and this would be equivalent to audio clipping. If you resort to the brightness control to adjust the peak luminance, you have reached the point in a display's life requiring a thorough functional review.

A CRT display has specifications that indicate a functional range over which operation is possible. A facility may desire less range because of ambient conditions or viewing preferences. However, the points where black and peak luminances are set should be well defined and maintained. These two end points, black and peak white, are the luminance range over which all the presentation image values will be mapped from the pre-DAC side.

9.2 Window Width and Window Level

Window width (window) and window level (level) is a portal from 16 bits of image data per pixel to 8 bits per pixel on the display, crossing the DAC divide between the two worlds. This is not a direct mapping of all the values in 16 bits being correlated to 8 bits so that each incremental step of 256 (8 bits) equals a block of 256 steps of 65,536 (16 bits). The window width can be as wide or as narrow as selected from the total steps available, as depicted in Fig. 9.1 with two different window widths. If 4096 sequential steps are selected as the window width, then the hardware LUT will map this range to 256 steps (8 bits). However, this does not define where the end points are located, which is where window level comes in.

Window level does this as a pointer, indicating the midpoint of the range selected. In the above example, the window level can be selected anywhere that 4096 sequential digital steps can be taken from 65,536. A window level of 2048 would put the steps between 0 and 4095 (4096 steps including zero). Shifting the level upward (brighter image content) moves the 4096 window steps into brighter tones, which would again be mapped to the display's 256 steps and luminance range. The window level determines both the starting point and the

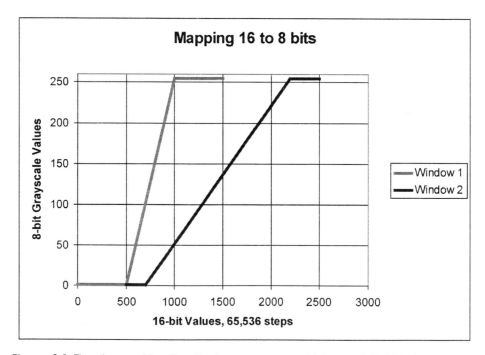

Figure 9.1 The slope of the line that encompasses N steps of 65,536 defines window width. Window 1 has a width of 500 to 1000 and window 2 is 700 to 2048. The window level would be the midpoint of their respective widths. In each case the slope is referenced to the 8-bit grayscale values. The actual conversion in the digital world would take place in a hardware lookup table.

end point of the selected window width to be viewed. Together the brightness and contrast on a display appear to equate to this, but only figuratively since they represent fixed operating parameters. It appears that brightness would also move a pointer from what happens to the image, but this is short lived because the display's physical limits are encountered and the lower gray tones are lost in addition to the DICOM calibration becoming corrupted. A reduction in display contrast will only bring down the peak luminance, which reduces the dynamic range and the number of JNDs generated. Initially this would appear to be equal to a narrowing of the window, but this just makes the display image less useful.

The mapping of 4096 digital steps into 256 is a few steps defining many, squeezing more into less space numerically. But if 4096 steps were equal to a delta luminance of only a few candelas, then 256 digital steps over 272 cd/m^2 (80 fL) would be an expansion of the tonal information as illustrated in Fig. 9.2. Whatever information was locked into those 4096 steps just got easier to see over a much larger luminance range (more JNDs are possible). So as the window is narrowed, an increasingly smaller sample of the total range available is taken and passed on to the display's fixed tonal range, expanding the luminance ratio representing the window. Going in the other direction, expanding the window width increasingly reduces the ability to see small tonal transitions as the tonal range of the native image exceeds the displays. The tonal content is compressed as more and more tonal values become closer to each other and are assigned to the same luminance value on the display. Also keep in mind that the tonal values for each pixel, below and above the end points of the window width, default to black and peak white, respectively. This causes some unusual image reversals to occur as brighter areas are selected.

Moving the window level into brighter areas such as those represented by bone makes the image darker, the inverse of what one would expect. These brighter areas are now being mapped into the display's range of 1.7 cd/m^2 (0.5 fL) to 272 cd/m^2 (80 fL) and all pixel tonal values below the window are now black. This makes the overall image appear much darker because an increasingly larger percentage of the total image (by individual pixel) is now represented by black. A range between air and body fat maps more pixels closer to peak luminance, so that what is normally the darkest image is now predominantly bright.

Again, the benefit of window and level is in the ability to map a selected range of tonal information and fine-tune it so that optimum viewing is realized, i.e., low-contrast areas are enhanced by spreading them over a larger luminance range on the display. The ability to see tonal transitions is limited to far less than 65,536 steps (16 bits), and the ability to select window and level for that information is the key to unlocking it in much the same way a hot light or a black mask would be used.

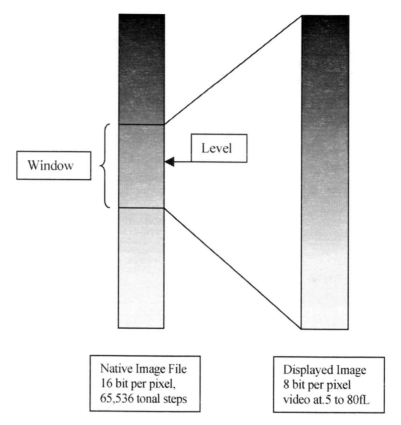

Figure 9.2 Selected window width and level from native image mapped to CRT display.

This description is intended to build a general understanding and not be modality specific. In computed tomography (CT), the numbers are referred to as Hounsfield units and starting at -1024 for air, with -100 for fat, water at 0, muscle at 100, and bone at 500.[1] Any other image source, including a digitized x ray at 16 bits, would provide the same flexibility to expand or compress a selected range of tonal values on a display device. The important thing is to not use the display's controls to achieve this; they are not the same. Reference 1 is an excellent source of additional background information on this subject. Another reference by Pomeranz[2] is also recommended.

References

1. T. Gillespy III and A. Rowberg, *J. of Digital Imaging,* **6**(3) 151–163 (1993).
2. S.M. Pomeranz, C.S. White, T.L. Krebs, B. Daly, S.A. Sukumar, F. Hooper and E.L. Siegel, "Liver and bone window settings for soft-copy interpretation of chest and abdominal CT," *Am. J. Rad,* **174**(2), pp. 311–314 (2002).

Chapter 10

OVERVIEW OF CRT RASTER DISPLAY

Today's modern computer display and HDTV rely on the same fundamentals that materialized from the first experimental television designs. The technology at the time, i.e., vacuum tubes, dictated the limits of performance that could be achieved. Early mainframe computer terminals, known as ASCII terminals, mimicked television refresh rates, with the United States at 60 Hz and Europe at 50 Hz. This required long, persistent phosphors to minimize flicker, which are typically not very efficient. Phosphors that were efficient with reasonable persistence were green and amber. With the desire to emulate the printed page in appearance came the realization that flicker that could be ignored on a B&W TV could not be ignored when reading black text on a white field. Increasing the refresh rate (vertical scan rate) to minimize flicker also increases the demand on the horizontal rate. The first major increase was from 15 kHz (TV 15,750 Hz actual) to 31.5 kHz, and this was considered leading-edge technology. Today, a 5-megapixel display operates at around 180 kHz and a 2-megapixel landscape at up to 105 kHz. In portrait orientation, a 2-megapixel display is at 120 kHz. In the early 1980s this would have been thinkable only on paper for commercial displays.

Raster-scanned displays require timing information for the horizontal and vertical rates so that the video appears at the correct location on the screen. All three can be combined into what is referred to as composite video, a single connection typical of procedural playback monitors. The display then separates them into their respective components through tuned circuits that strip them apart. The next level up is separate video and composite sync. Isolating the video from the sync is better for maintaining a clean video signal. At the higher frequencies, separate sync and video with quality shielding is best. A term called sync on green applies to both monochrome and color displays that can also strip sync out of the green input channel. Typically there is a logic chip that will look for separate sync at their inputs and if none is detected, it will look on the green channel; the hierarchy would first default to separate syncs.

The industry-standard high-density 15-pin VGA connector on the PC and/or the display provides the respective signals separately. The twist-and-lock (bayonet) type is called a BNC and is by design a single-wire connector. The BNC type will provide maximum shielding and isolation.

10.1 Sync Signals

The sync signals (input source) only control when the display circuits start and stop their respective sweep waveform. The display contains the oscillator circuits that generate the ramps that sweep the beam from the top to bottom and left to right. Today's displays utilize phase-lock-loop (PLL) control circuits that constantly compare the running sweep circuit with the timing pulses (input) and generate a corrective signal with each cycle. That is why vertical and horizontal sync controls have not been on TVs or displays for a long time (or are out of sight).

Sync signals are analog and the term associated with their connection is transistor-to-transistor logic (TTL). The standard calls for a 1- to 5-V pulse, which acts like a trigger to the receiving transistor. The pulse is represented by a square wave, meaning there are two logic levels. One is high and one is low, with a rise and fall transition. This puts minimums on the video card for the pulse duration so that it can be recognized by the display. Truncating the pulse width provides more time for the card to do other functions, but it can cause a loss of sync or unstable condition for the PLL circuit.

The leading edge of a sync pulse is called the back porch; it represents the end of the line just written (horizontal) or the end of the frame (vertical). The trailing edge is the front porch, which is starting a new line or frame (Fig. 10.1). In order to stabilize circuits going into a new frame or line, blank lines and blank pixels can be found on all the edges, i.e., outside the active video area. This varies with video cards, and in some cases a few shortcuts in timing can cause problems to show up on the display. The front and back porch define the raster, which is the area within which video can be written. A designer will typically express this in terms of lines and pixels as opposed to fractions of a second. The active video within the raster is located by the display's size

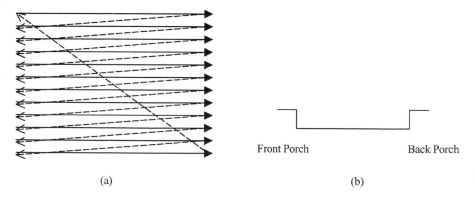

         (a)   (b)

Figure 10.1 (a) Vertical sync pulse occurs after each frame is written; dashed lines are retrace lines, solid lines are written lines. (b) Horizontal sync pulse with video content that falls between the front and back porch for each line.

and centering controls. The video cannot be larger than the raster area and the number of lines and pixels allocated as blank represents the limits of positional adjustment.

If the raster is not well centered on the screen, the centering adjustment for the video will not be able to make corrections. The controls run out of range and cause video foldover, in which the left edge of the video wraps around to the right side of the screen when the video is moved to the left. A phase difference between the video source and display is not uncommon, and when it is coupled with a limited adjustment range it will prevent the image from being centered. A number of commercial cards do provide a GUI interface to adjust for a phase shift, but this does not correct for the absence of a sufficient number of blanked pixels and lines. Monitors do have an internal phase adjustment, but it is not typically a user control.

The specified pixel format (addressable) does not include the blanked lines and pixels. However, by turning the brightness up, the raster edge can be seen. The term *background raster* applies to the luminance level of the raster area, which is also the black level within the active video.

Blanking refers to cutting off the video (no electron flow from the cathode) to black. The blanked lines and pixels are off because an applied voltage called video blanking blocks the video circuit. During retrace when the beam is returned to the left edge or top of the CRT, the video amplifier is forced off so that no electrons flow to the phosphor based on the commanded video drive. This occurs during the respective sync pulse, i.e., a minimum pulse width is required from the card. The sync circuits provide the blanking trigger to the video amplifier during retrace. The ability to see background raster outside the active video area is the result of electron flow that occurs by virtue of the brightness setting (black level).

10.2 Video Signal Distortions

The video signal is an analog voltage that changes with the luminance information desired. It remains isolated throughout the display to preserve its integrity. Terms associated with interference are called smearing, ghosting, and ringing. In addition, the frequencies associated with the vertical and horizontal sync circuits can corrupt the video if they are brought into close proximity within the display. Circuit layout and wire dressing (positioning) are critical elements of a CRT display. Every wire or pathway on a printed wire board (PWB) is a potential antenna.

In general, they are all referred to as artifacts in the image. All of these artifacts should be isolated and removed during the design phase. Production in volume introduces a larger population of possible tolerance buildup combinations, which also need to be addressed in preproduction and continuing engineering support. The video circuit is not the only pathway for interference; the deflection circuits and yoke can also cause uneven luminance without penetrating the video path.

A luminance distortion called jail bars consists of vertically oriented lines and shows up on the left side, usually within the first few inches. These are sinusoidal fluctuations in luminance. From a few to many can appear and their interval is an indication to the designer that the horizontal and vertical coils on the yoke are interfering with each other (cross talk). During each frame, the horizontal is retracing for each line, including blanked lines, while the vertical is doing one ramp. The horizontal ramp (also called sweep) is very quickly reversed in a fraction of the time represented by the ramp when writing a line. The sudden reversal causes inductance, which needs to be damped out before the next line starts (active area). If this is not accomplished quickly, the inducted energy in the yoke shows up on the screen as jail bars.

10.3 High-Voltage Source

There are two avenues here for the designer. Televisions, computer displays, and 1k-line medical displays can be expected to have a flyback transformer as the source of anode voltage. Four- and 5-megapixel (2k/2.5k-line) displays can use a regulated high-voltage power supply or regulated flyback.

Televisions and computer displays (commercial products) can be unregulated without causing image problems within their intended use. Poor regulation can, however, cause nonuniformity of luminance and unstable video size with rapid changes in image content, such as running a CINE loop. Adding regulation to a flyback transformer stabilizes luminance and size under the harsher conditions typical of medical imaging. This is accomplished with pulse-width-modulation of the primary windings of the flyback transformer. A control chip senses the beam current being absorbed at the view screen and alters the horizontal retrace pulse time to the flyback independently of the horizontal sweep current going to the yoke. Because the horizontal sync circuit is the source for both, a complete decoupling cannot be achieved. The designer's flexibility does have limits.

A separately regulated high-voltage power supply operates independently of the horizontal and will provide the best overall control. However, it represents a major increase in cost over a regulated flyback system for improving high voltage to better than a 0.5% maximum size change when alternating between full white and black screens. In medical and commercial imaging, this situation is not typical of normal use. A properly sized flyback transformer and controller circuit can be expected to correct for any sudden change in current flow within two to three frames at 70-Hz vertical refresh rate.

10.4 Interlaced and Sequential Scan

Sequential scan is the most common format for computer and medical displays. It is also referred to as progressive scan. Televisions are interlaced for NTSC (520 lines at 60 Hz) and PAL (600 lines at 50 Hz) broadcast signals that also apply to cable. The high definition television (HDTV) format is intended to be sequential at 1k lines. It becomes a backward compatibility issue for HDTV to accept NTSC at 520 lines interlaced in addition to switching from analog to digital broadcasting.

An interlaced scan is made up of two fields to form one frame. They can be thought of as odd and even lines starting with the first field (odd) and writing the lines from top to bottom. When vertical retrace brings the beam back to the top, an offset is incorporated that makes the second field (even) fall between the odd lines. At 70 Hz refresh, each field is scanned 35 times per second for a net refresh rate of 70 Hz. Interlacing permits a higher line count without going to higher horizontal rates and video bandwidth to support the faster writing speed. It will also reduce the perception of flicker when viewed at a distance. Up close, interlaced displays reveal the problem areas that can occur.

Interlaced scan is common in fluoroscopy because of the close connection with TV camera systems. Recordings onto VCR tape formats also followed the commercial industry and perpetuated the use of interlaced display systems. The current generation of fluoroscopy has moved to sequential scans from either a camera upgrade or a digital sensor system. The availability of scan converters can remove potential hardware compatibility problems between old and new at either end of the image path.

Magnetic distortions and unstable sync signals (especially from VCR decks) can cause the spacing between interlaced fields to become uneven. The term line pairing refers to the evenness of the spacing. Ideally, the lines are balanced 50/50 from top to bottom, i.e., evenly spaced. Reality is closer to 60/40 and this can vary from top to bottom. Eye movements and head movements can cause the image to break up into horizontal bands. Multisync displays optimized for sequential scanning do not generally deal well with interlaced signals and suffer line-pairing distortions.

Color displays capable of accepting an interlaced signal will generally not exhibit the same visible degree of distortion as monochrome. The larger pixel sizes and the inherent structure of the shadow mask will hide pairing problems that are otherwise visible on a monochrome. The lines could be on top of each other (odd–even frame overlapping) in the bottom third of the screen and be objectionable on monochrome but not even noticed on a color display.

10.5 Geometric Distortions

CRT displays are subject to geometric distortion because the electron beam has to travel in a magnetic environment. This is the result of not just the deflection yoke, but also the earth's magnetic field, which varies in strength and orientation around the globe. What is square to the bezel in the Northern Hemisphere will be rotated counterclockwise and moved to the left in the Southern Hemisphere. Incorporating user control to compensate for positional errors is standard, but there are unusual cases where the control authority is exceeded. A facility's other equipment or higher-intensity magnetic fields within the earth's crust (i.e., lodestone deposits) can cause this. The obvious MRI source is easily avoided, but there are other, not so obvious sources in many buildings.

The power for a commercial building is contained in conduits running through walls and ceilings. An elevator shaft provides a central location for wide power distribution. Large conduits carrying 3-phase 208 V ac for elevators are also split into individual phases for lighting grids. A diagnostic reading room sharing a common wall with the elevator shaft could experience large distortions caused by the fields around the conduit. Support columns using pipe that is anchored into the footing of a building act like funnels, concentrating the magnetic energy and distorting the natural fields around the columns. In both instances, rotating the display 90 deg will reveal whether a local source is the problem. If no change is observed, the display unit should be moved 10 feet away to confirm that there is no change and that the display is not locally influenced.

Color CRTs contain internal shielding against magnetic flux lines to prevent color purity problems. Very small distortions in the multibeam trajectory would be noticed immediately in the form of color variations. Geometric distortions would be secondary to purity for objectionable image quality in color. Monochrome, on the other hand, with a single beam and phosphor, will not have purity issues, but because monochrome CRTs do not contain internal shielding, the influence on geometry will be greater unless shielding external to the CRT is utilized.

A quality display design will use neutral field deflection yokes within cost limits and intrinsic performance trade-offs. Their purpose is to cancel the radiated energy of the yoke so that adjacent displays and/or sensitive electronic equipment are not adversely influenced. The yoke designer can provide this benefit in a number of ways using added coils (bucking coils) to oppose radiated energy. A workstation using two heads, with one being color, has the most potential for corruption. As noted earlier, color CRTs have internal shielding, but if the yoke is not neutral, the radiated energy can distort the geometry of a color or monochrome display on the side closest to the color. Ferrous and nonferrous metal chassis parts and cabinets (including coated plastic) do not block magnetic energy. Simply moving the two displays apart will confirm this problem. A special material called Mu metal does absorb magnetic forces, but it is a very expensive solution and is used sparingly only in critical areas, such as around the electron gun structure. Refer to Fig. 10.2(a)–(f) for the common geometry distortions as described below.

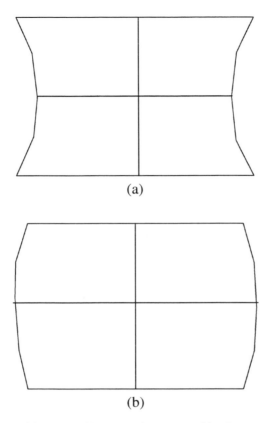

(a)

(b)

Figure 10.2 (a) Pincushion distortions can be symmetrical or nonsymmetrical from left to right side. (b) Barrrel distortions are the opposite of the pincushion and can be nonsymmetrical.

A pincushion distortion is normally associated with the left and right edge representing the video width. The top and bottom edges can also have a similar appearance. Yokes are designed so that they have some pin to the uncorrected geometry. Correction can be accomplished with magnets applied to the yoke housing in a basic system without electronic pincushion correction, or a combination of both. An electronic pincushion would adjust the width by modifying the horizontal sawtooth waveform. A digitally controlled display would segment the screen and calculate corrections to the horizontal width for each segment in real time. Increasing the number of segments yields an increasingly finer degree of correction. An analog correction would be adjustments (using pots) to generate a best fit. Magnets can also be added to the CRT funnel area with adhesive as a last resort.

High-quality yokes require the fewest magnets for correction on all edges. As yoke quality goes down, the number of magnets increases. This is detrimental to the image quality because magnets pull the beam apart in addition to

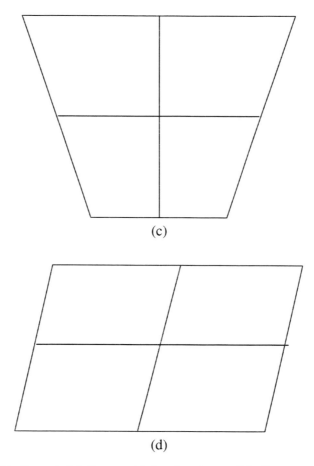

(c)

(d)

Figure 10.2 Continued. (c) Trapezoidal or keystone distortions can be nonsymmetrical left to right side. (d) Orthogonal is created by a yoke construction problem in the relationship between the vertical and horizontal windings causing the vertical and horizontal centerlines are no longer perpendicular to each other.

bending it. The combination of a poor yoke and the added magnets is a downward spiral in performance that should be avoided.

A barrel distortion is the opposite of a pincushion and can be thought of as pincushion overcorrection. In a basic system, magnets would need to be removed or rotated to reduce their influence.

A trapezoidal (keystone) distortion is caused by a difference between opposing yoke windings. The trapezoid can be symmetrical or nonsymmetrical. Electronic correction under digital control has the ability to provide symmetrical compensation and trapezoidal balance.

An orthogonal is a yoke manufacturing error that causes the relationship between the horizontal and vertical windings to be misaligned. The visual cue is the intersection of the vertical and horizontal lines at screen center. Their intersection will be an angle other than 90 deg. Attempts to adjust for this problem

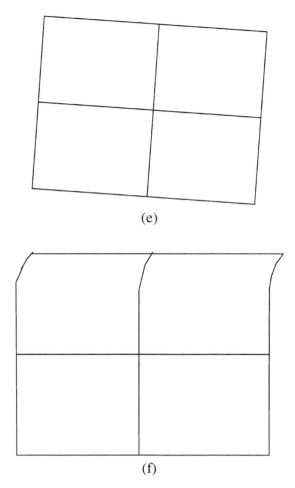

(e)

(f)

Figure 10.2 Continued. (e) Tilt or rotation is a hemispheric distortion adjusted by user controls; the geometry is otherwise correct. (f) Hook distortion can be caused by a design issue or a poor quality video card with insufficient blanking time for the display.

induces other distortions in image quality. In a perfect yoke, the beam at screen center is at the magnetic center of both windings. Disparity between the windings means the beam can no longer remain at the magnetic center of both. The more severe the disparity, the worse the net result.

Tilt is a simple rotational change in the entire image. At the time of manufacture, the yoke must be installed and aligned to the CRT. It is held in place by a mechanical clamp on the CRT neck and hot glue at the funnel. A display rotation that is due to earth's magnetic fields should be within the corrective range of a tilt adjustment. A rotation coil can be integrated into the yoke housing or attached to the CRT funnel. This is nothing more than a loop made from a continuous wire with a small current applied.

A hook is found at the top of the vertical lines, with the upper left corner typically being the most severe area. It is caused by cross talk between the vertical and horizontal windings at the juncture of the retrace for both sweeps; i.e., both magnetic fields have been collapsed (reversed) to initiate the next frame. If insufficient time is available to stabilize the horizontal sweep circuits (which include the yoke windings), inductive energy from the vertical and collapsing horizontal fields will cause the hook. Video cards that do not provide blanking time at the beginning of a frame can cause this on an otherwise good-quality display.

Inner line distortion is primarily a yoke winding distribution problem and/or a CRT with a compound internal radius that cannot be compensated for by the yoke. A compound radius changes the throw distance (electron gun to screen) for the beam from one radius to another, and this can occur on both the horizontal and vertical axes of the CRT at different rates of change. From a manufacturing perspective, you find a yoke that minimizes it and yields the fewest yoke rejects. The distortion typically shows up between the second and fourth horizontal line of a SMPTE pattern grid.

10.6 Digital versus Analog Control

Very few displays can be found today with an analog potentiometer controlling anything. Those with a knob and shaft are usually attached to a counter, and are part of an up/down digital circuit. In the world of multisync displays, using 35 or more potentiometers to set up a display run counter to manufacturing simplicity and ease of maintenance. Providing digital user controls as the interface results in better consistency and predictability of outcome, but this is not to say a display is controlled digitally.

Up/down counters provide control voltages to analog circuits. The actual waveform generation and final outputs remain in the analog world. This limits the ability to fine tune a circuit in relative terms as in a full digital implementation and usually means there are internal factory adjustments (potentiometers). A full digital control architecture would include a microprocessor that controls all waveform generation based on analyzing the input signals and user preferences. Custom ASIC technology can also be employed to carry out repetitive routines monitored by the processor. By controlling waveform generation in the digital world, intentional distortions of a waveform can be achieved that would otherwise not be possible in an analog design. This provides better performance matching among the CRT, yoke, and circuit tolerance variations.

Digital control provides the manufacturer with the ability to interface with the circuits via a communications port such as an RS232. Service software, which is an extension of the factory-built software, provides digital values for control elements that are not only repeatable but can be downloaded in one step. Control elements that are interactive, meaning they influence each other, such as size and linearity, can be linked within limits and autoadjusted. A manufacturing process would utilize script files to sequence setup procedures and prompt operators throughout the process. Setup software can also provide adjustment limits that when exceeded would indicate possible problems. Tracking final values and downloading them provides a concise as-built record tied to the display; service technicians can easily refer back to as-shipped data and compare them with values observed in the field.

Microprocessor control can also provide tracking of faults so that if a unit fails in the analog world, the microprocessor can log it. In general, four to six key points are sufficient to isolate a failure. An alternative to a single micro for failure detection is to utilize flash memory chips on major circuit boards, providing even greater detailed analysis potential.

In summary, medical displays are best served by digital control architectures. When implemented correctly, they add to the overall flexibility of the display to function properly with various workstation configurations, i.e., video card variations.

Chapter 11

IMAGE QUALITY CONTROL AND MAINTAINING PERFORMANCE

An understanding of phosphor and cathode aging leads to the obvious assumption that things change over time. Maintaining, as-new performance cannot be isolated to peak luminance level criteria while the image quality, such as contrast modulation, deteriorates in real terms. Whether automatic compensation or scheduled service cycles using human intervention are used to maintain a display, the end result is the same. It is up to the end user to evaluate the facility's needs and the cost of ownership associated with the different vendor solutions.

Internal compensation can either address the total system response, including both cathode and phosphor aging, or the cathode only. A circuit that compares volts driven for cathode current produced and constantly adjusts the drive (video gain) can provide the latter. The circuit would have the as-new values as a reference point for calculating the required adjustment. This approach ignores the phosphor aging contribution. By using P45, which ages very slowly under the harshest of operating conditions, this element is minimized and can be ignored in the short term as long as routine calibration cycles are performed. A blended phosphor such as PC104 would cause an error to accumulate in a relatively short time.

A solution including phosphor aging requires a luminance sensor. This can be achieved using internal photometers integrated into the display that would provide hands-free calibration checks. A number of approaches have been used in the past that place the sensor just under the bezel and detect black-level settings well, but not peak luminance. The phosphor under the sensor sees very little electron energy in normal operation and would not be aging equally with the screen center.

Being under the bezel also shields some of the ambient light that would be part of all readings but is particularly significant for black-level settings. A correlation can be made to ambient light from the CRT edge area, but this represents a very small sample area that could be adversely influenced by a localized shadow. An alternative approach is a sensor located on the CRT funnel, which has a view of the entire screen area from the back. This provides the ability to read black-level and peak luminance and to be correlated to the DICOM grayscale standard display function parameters that call out a test square with 20% surround luminance. In addition, an ambient measurement inclusive of the full screen can also be made and used as a reference.

It is possible to measure luminance from the funnel because the aluminum backing on the phosphor has microscopic pinholes. The CRT manufacturing process that bakes out the moisture from the phosphor screen causes these pin-holes. Luminance energy from the phosphor and ambient light penetrate into the funnel area, albeit significantly attenuated, and can be measured by a quality photometer. In contrast, displays with internal compensation circuits would still require a hand-held meter for testing DICOM conformance. The internal compensation approach would compensate black-level and peak luminance using the correlation of drive to current for the time between scheduled calibrations.

11.1 Bundled Quality Control Solutions

Bundled quality control solutions are normally associated with a medical video card vendor's software offering. A number of major original equipment man-ufacturers (OEMs) purchase and integrate them within their overall package. They would include test pattern generation in compliance with the DICOM grayscale standard display function to generate the LUT, a library of industry test patterns (such as a SMPTE pattern), and readout of results (i.e., compli-ance record). Software hooks for network communications so that results can be centrally archived should also be part of any facility-wide solution.

Software from nonvideo card vendors is another approach to quality control, but it must take a more general path to be compatible with the larger population of video cards. Their benefit is predominantly linked to commercial video cards that lack the features of a medical card. The LUT and selection of window and leveling would be accomplished in software prior to the video card. The vendor would also have to provide test pattern generation and a hand-held photometer for calibrating the software-based LUT to the display. The photometer would be connected to a serial or universal serial bus (USB) port on the workstation. Dedicated medical cards provide their own port; a connector such as a PS2 is typical.

Neither approach is dependent on the display for feedback, nor does it com-municate with the display. There is a need in both cases for the display to be set up correctly in order for the calibration to be beneficial. Performance differ-ences between models and within models that are due to the limits of normal use that the calibration must work within. Whatever the dynamic range is, the number of just noticeable differences produced will be influenced by it.

Displays that automatically calibrate their end points (black and peak white) reduce the potential error from calibration software trying to adjust a display that is out of specification. However, there is still no feedback between the dis-play and calibration software that can provide greater functional detail. The use of full digital control allows communication between the display and calibra-tion software. With the right software tool set and internal photometer, a true hands-free calibration and verification can be accomplished under network control or local request if an image is of questionable quality. This last configuration requires a coordinated effort between the video card source and the display manufacturer.

11.2 IMAGE Smiths* VeriLUM

IMAGE Smiths VeriLUM is a front-end software calibration kit that includes a photometer and software compatible with most PC-based workstations and recognized video graphic cards. The calibration routine follows the DICOM standard procedure, with a test square centered within the video equal to 10% of the active area, and the surround is set to 20% of maximum luminance. Calibration test functions are included for both monochrome and color CRT displays as well as support for flat panels.

The results can be plotted and the built-in SMPTE pattern can confirm that the 5% and 95% squares have equal perceptibility. Gamma correction can be turned off and on to observe the difference. A number of commercial video cards are compatible with VeriLUM and can import the LUT scaling, providing faster throughput of image data.

As with all calibrations, the black level and peak white of the display should be set first. Video drive levels for black and peak white can be selected from the user interface. The photometer is a high-quality sensor that interfaces via a serial port automatically detected by the software with either a serial or USB connector; the software will automatically locate the port selected. For more information: www.image-smiths.com.

11.3 DOME* Imaging TQA

DOME's TQA (total quality assurance) functions with a hand-held photometer connected directly to the video card. A full library of functions in accordance with DICOM is provided. As noted earlier, the display should be set up correctly for black level and peak white before a calibration cycle is initiated. In its standard hardware configuration TQA has no way of adjusting the display's dynamic range. Support personnel must verify this. The photometer and built-in test patterns support this function, but the display controls must be accessed for correction.

DOME TQA along with a library of tools for system integrators, comes close to providing the ultimate solution. The choice of display and its ability to communicate with TQA is the last limiting factor for CRT displays.

---

*IMAGE Smiths and DOME imaging are trademarks of their respective companies.

Appendix

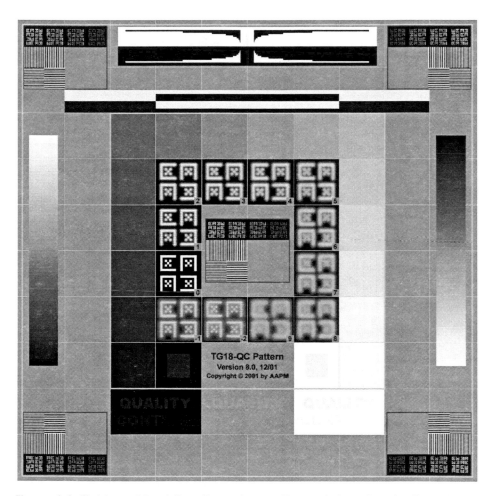

Figure A.1 Eight- and ten-bit patterns for quality control and evaluation of soft-copy displays developed by the American Association of Physicists in Medicine, Task Group 18. (Image courtesy of AAPM.)

Index

 **Kenneth D. Compton** received his BS degree from Moravian College in 1966 and has been with Clinton Electronics for 16 years, working with display manufacturer's who use cathode ray tube technology in commercial and medical imaging applications. Over the last nine years, Mr. Compton has focused on medical imaging and the development of medical displays. His on going involvement with various medical research organizations has brought the knowledge of the end user into the design phase of a display system to enhance the quality of softcopy. Mr. Compton is an active member of SPIE and SCAR and participates in panel discussions on display related questions. He has published more than 15 papers on imaging and display technology; his speaking experience includes symposium and formal training environments at HealthTech, SPIE Medical Imaging, and IWDM2000, in addition to internal training for Clinton Electronics and its distributors. Mr. Compton has served as part of the working group on Digital Mammography sponsored by the Office of Women's Health, and has been an industry liaison, consultant, and author for the AAPM Task Group 18.